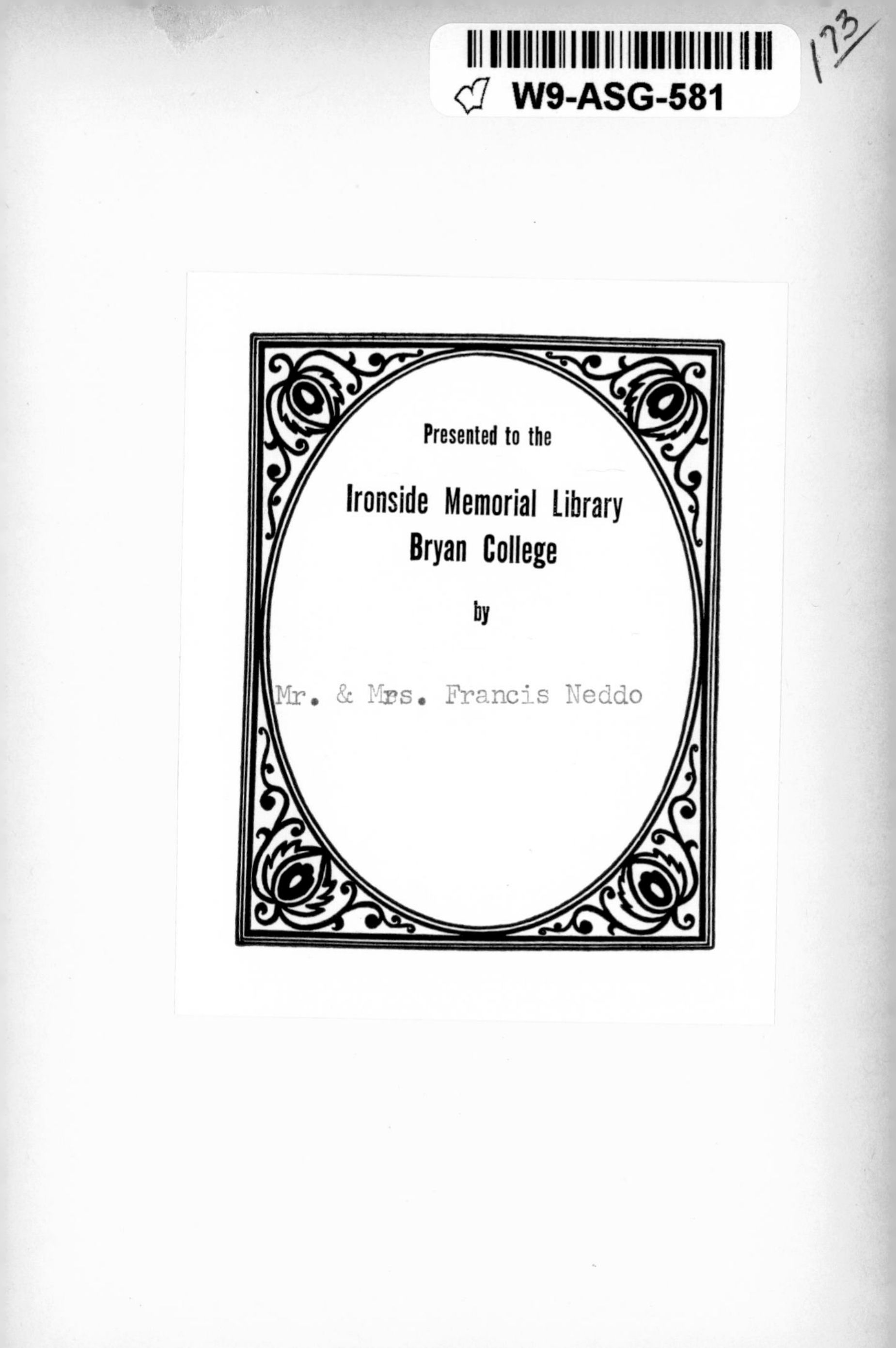
W9-ASG-581
173
Presented to the
Ironside Memorial Library
Bryan College
by
Mr. & Mrs. Francis Neddo

Is Christ for John Smith?

Is Christ for John Smith?

Edited by John A. Ishee

BROADMAN PRESS
Nashville, Tennessee

422–514
DEWEY DECIMAL CLASSIFICATION NUMBER: 248.5
Library of Congress Catalog Card Number: 68–20677
Printed in the United States of America
20.AL68KSP

PREFACE

Nicodemus, the woman at the well in Samaria, Zacchaeus—these and many more were persons who experienced direct encounter with Jesus. He offered the same faith and hope to all of them, yet his approach to each person was unique. He possessed the keen ability to analyze a situation and approach the person in the most effective way to meet his needs.

Obviously, none of us is able to equate our witnessing with the effectiveness of Jesus' witnessing. Jesus does expect us, however, to use in the most effective manner the witnessing ability we do possess.

Witnessing is dynamic. It is impossible to discover one approach to be used by all Christian witnesses in all witnessing situations. The dynamics of witnessing arise from differences in the person engaged in witnessing, differences in the person to whom the witness is given, and the environment in which the witnessing may occur. This book seeks to recognize these variables. Therefore, the three analyses of each case or situation in the book, while containing many similarities, will be different. The "analysts" were asked to "speak their minds" on each case. This they have done. The editor has sought to maintain the originality of each analyst. If contradictions are apparent, they arise from these variables.

This book is designed to help you become a more effective witness. In each chapter, there is a case situation followed by analyses by Kenneth L. Chafin, Herschel H. Hobbs, and G. Avery Lee. While many insights are given for each situation, no attempt has been made to give "the last word" on how to witness. You, the reader, are challenged to think of how you would witness in each case. Perhaps, after reading the book, you will discuss with other Christians other factors to consider and actions to take in witnessing to the persons dealt with in this book.

Teamwork on the part of all contributors aided immensely in the production of this book. A word of appreciation is due to Raymond M. Rigdon, who initiated the idea for the project. Mrs. Ruby McMillin made numerous structural improvements. If this small volume can help Christians to witness more effectively in our strategic age, we shall all have our reward.

JOHN A. ISHEE

CONTENTS

1. "I've Got My Eyes on Better Things"
   (By John Warren Steen) ____ 9
   How to Win This Person to Christ
   (By Kenneth Chafin, Herschel Hobbs, G. Avery Lee) ____ 15

2. "I Just Don't Need What You've Got to Sell"
   (By Jack D. Sanford) ____ 24
   How to Win This Person to Christ
   (By Kenneth Chafin, Herschel Hobbs, G. Avery Lee) ____ 30

3. "All This Repentance Stuff Is Not for Me"
   (By William L. Self) ____ 38
   How to Win This Person to Christ
   (By Kenneth Chafin, Herschel Hobbs, G. Avery Lee) ____ 44

4. "Forget About the Money-Grabbing Churches"
   (By Harold E. Dye) ____ 52
   How to Win This Person to Christ
   (By Kenneth Chafin, Herschel Hobbs, G. Avery Lee) ____ 59

5. "I'm About at the End of My Rope"
(By Albert L. Meiburg) ______ 67
How to Win This Person to Christ
(By Kenneth Chafin, Herschel Hobbs, G. Avery Lee) ______ 73
6. "Christianity Is the White Man's Religion"
(By W. T. Moore) ______ 80
How to Win This Person to Christ
(By Kenneth Chafin, Herschel Hobbs, G. Avery Lee) ______ 86
7. "Chaplain, What Really Bugs Me Is Being Alone"
(By Clifford Ingle) ______ 94
How to Win This Person to Christ
(By Kenneth Chafin, Herschel Hobbs, G. Avery Lee) ______ 98
8. "What's God Ever Done for Me?"
(By John D. Hendrix) ______ 106
How to Win This Person to Christ
(By Kenneth Chafin, Herschel Hobbs, G. Avery Lee) ______ 111
9. "If They Really Knew"
(By Albert L. Meiburg) ______ 119
How to Win This Person to Christ
(By Kenneth Chafin, Herschel Hobbs, G. Avery Lee) ______ 122
Who's Who ______ 128

1

"I've Got My Eyes on Better Things"

John Warren Steen, Jr.

Jerry Hinson, a telephone lineman in his early twenties, usually keeps his feelings buried under a mask of confident calm. Today, he is scared and shows it, biting his lower lip. He is waiting in the lounge outside the maternity wing of a hospital. Jerry's wife has just gone into the labor room. He is sitting with another expectant father. Although he is a friendly person, Jerry is usually not very communicative. Today he is more talkative, and he asks, "Been here before?"

"No. This is my first time."

Jerry eagerly responds. "It's my first time, too, and I have to admit I'm scared. I thought the last several months went slow, but this is really a drag."

"I hope your wife wasn't scared. Mine wasn't."

"Mine wasn't either, but I wish I had something to calm myself down right now."

The new friend inquires, "Why are you so worried?"

"One of the old-timers I work with really scared me this morning. He said that his wife screamed so much in labor that she lost her voice for two days. She bit her lips so badly, he said, that it took three weeks for them to heal."

"Sounds to me like he's fifty years behind times. People look on birth now as a normal part of nature, not some torture to be endured."

"That's what her doctor said all along. My wife's not worried. But this old fellow today really got me shook up."

"Her doctor is a specialist and will give her the sedation she needs to take the edge off her pain. If she's not worried or scared when she goes in, she won't have any trouble."

Jerry leans back, relaxed. "She has a lot of faith."

"That's good. How about yourself?"

Jerry smiles slyly. "I have hopes for a nice big boy. I want him to be healthy. That's all I care about. No matter how much the doctor charges, it will be worth it to have a fine healthy baby of our own."

"Speaking of charges, I had no idea it would be so expensive to have a baby."

"Me either. I had been thinking of the income tax deduction and what a help that would be. But it is going to take more than that to pay for baby furniture, clothes, bills, and stuff like that."

The new friend offers a light for Jerry's cigarette and says, "I am not worried about any of that, really. If my wife comes through all right and the baby is OK, that is all I pray for."

At the mention of prayer, Jerry gets up and walks down the corridor, blowing smoke. Later he returns, as if looking for someone. The friend says, "Do you expect anybody else to come by and wait with you?"

"No. I was just looking to see if any new customers had come in. All the fellows I work with have children of their own. They don't think it's so special that we are having a baby."

"I don't have anybody either. My pastor said he would drop by, if I called to let him know when we came to the hospital, but I . . ."

Jerry interrupts. "You can do it, if you want to. But if you get some 'Holy Joe' in here, I'm going down the hall."

"Are you running from religion?"

For a long time Jerry is silent, then he says, "I just don't have time for church. I work all day long climbing poles and going up under houses to work on telephone lines. I come home pretty tired out, and on Saturdays I work at a sporting goods shop."

"You've set a busy schedule for yourself."

"It's not just for myself. I want to provide for the baby. I've been trying to save up for him, but with my car payments what they are I haven't made much progress, just a little. But I want more. The best won't be too good for my baby."

The friend asked, "Do you like your work?"

"Does anybody like work?"

"Yes, I like mine. I'm an accountant, and I wouldn't swap jobs with anyone."

"Well, I like mine, too. But I would dump it in a minute if I could make more money. Sometimes, I think I'll take a civil service exam and see if I can better myself. Of course, I would hate to lose the years I have put in with the telephone company. I have built up some seniority, and I'm in line for a promotion. They gave me my job back when I got back from the Army, so I didn't lose any time. I thought of changing, but I like outside work. I'd die if I had to sit in an office all day. But I wish I got paid more. There's so much I want for myself and my family."

"My wife works and helps out with our income, but now that's a thing of the past."

"Mine did too. She taught school. But these Victorians on the school board made her quit when she started wearing maternity clothes. Man, we could have used those extra three or four months of salary."

The accountant asks, "Can you meet your obligations if you remain a lineman?"

"I've really got my eyes on better things," Jerry answers. "I plan to move up in the company. I've noticed how certain characters move ahead in my company. They have their ways."

"By kicking others out of the way?"

"No, I wouldn't do that unless a guy really deserved it. But I've noticed that the ones who get ahead are the ones who keep themselves in view of their supervisors and executives all the time. The fellows on their way up copy their bosses, all the way to their clothes and expressions of speech. It looks easy enough to try."

"You sound like you plan to succeed in business really trying."

"You're darn right. A guy has to be on the right escalator, the right transportation to the top."

"Do you think the rewards are worth all this trouble?"

"Don't kid yourself. The executives have their weekend cottages and their Cadillacs, and I don't see any of them giving them away. They're living it up. But I will be too."

"I'll give the "top brass" two years to notice me."

"Sounds like you are in a hurry."

"I wasted two years of my life in Vietnam, and I'm ready to live. I have a sports car and a color TV, neither paid for. But they're worth the payments and interest."

The other expectant father pulls his chair closer. "Listen, Friend, don't you have any more than these things to live for?"

"Sure, I live for the races. I'm a nut about speed. My wife says that she is a racetrack widow, but she'll just have to do without me. It's not often I go out with the boys for a beer. But every February, I head for Daytona Beach, and then I always go to Indianapolis for Memorial Day, and make as many of the others as I can."

"No, I mean something to live for, like church, or Christian principles, or hope of heaven."

Jerry pounds the armrest of his chair. "Pal, I told you I have no time for church."

"I'm not just talking about going to church, even though attendance at church means a lot in my life. I'm talking about faith, a foundation for . . ."

"With my background, maybe that foundation part is my trouble. I could never become a believer. My mother was a Protestant, but my father was a Catholic. They never took us to either church. You see, they quarreled about so many other things that they must have decided that church was *one* subject that was not worth the fire power. My home life was not too happy. I certainly hope to make a better one for my children."

"You can make it worthwhile. Why don't you try reading the Bible and discovering a faith for yourself?"

"I wouldn't know what the book's all about."

"You could go to Sunday School and church and learn."

"Negative. I've been in the United States Army, and I don't plan to get involved in anything else."

"Well, I was just making a suggestion, because you said you wanted a better life for your children than the mixed-up situation of your childhood. I certainly don't mean to put any pressure on you."

The permissive approach shocks Jerry into silence and brooding. The friend lets him think for a long time and then says, "This has been like taking a trip. You get to know people pretty well on a trip. We've gotten acquainted; in fact, to tell the truth, I feel like we are good friends."

Jerry says, "Yeah. I feel like I have gotten to know you. And I don't mind saying you seem more interested in my problems than any of the guys I work with. You're the kind of person a man could go to when he's in trouble."

"That's a very fine thing to say about anyone. I wish I deserved it. Jerry, I wish I could be of more help to you."

"You have been already. You helped me get over being scared."

The accountant adds, "I mean on a deeper level, with your religious questions." The words seem to scare Jerry back into his corner of silence. After a pause, the accountant adds, "This waiting is awful, isn't it?"

HOW TO WIN THIS PERSON TO CHRIST

Kenneth L. Chafin . . .

As you read about the individuals in this book you will probably come to the same conclusion that I did: These are not John Smiths, if we mean by that, average or typical. These individuals tend toward extremes. This is probably natural since we often think of a task in terms of the hardest part. While each individual is unique, there are certain principles, attitudes, and approaches which will be suggested which will have application with all individuals.

In each of the cases, I intend to state a principle which applies to the case but has a larger application. Then I intend to give my natural and honest, though very fallible response, with some suggestions as possible directions to begin witnessing. At the onset, this suggests that most effective witnessing involves a continuing relationship and that the one-visit approach which is successful is the exception and not the rule.

Principle.—There are no individuals whom we will meet who are outside God's love and concern.

There are people whom we will not like. Actually, I find myself responding negatively to some of the people in this book. But the principle is still valid. What I need to do in each case is to pray, "God, I know that you love this person and have a plan for his life. Help me to begin to see him as you do." Looking at individuals through God's eyes is a good first step in witnessing to them.

Jerry Hinson is quite typical of so many young married

adults. He is ambitious and has a plan for his life. So far, he has not discovered much dimension to life except as it relates to making money. However, in Jerry's plan he has given little thought to life's ultimate meaning, to his marriage, to this new relationship, to the child which is about to be born.

An initial contact can be made with a person at a crisis time, sometimes, which cannot be made at any other time. Undoubtedly, Jerry would not have talked to this individual as much as he did had it been a more casual contact.

It would be a mistake to try to push him into some sort of decision at this time. However, to use this waiting time as an effort to get to understand him would be very profitable. Wait with him for his baby. Congratulate him when it is born. Share with him some of your frustrations and also some of your ambitions for your child which is about to be born.

It seems that one of the clues in this case is the wife who is a Christian and a church member. Drop by the room and introduce yourself to the wife. This contact might be helpful. If there is an appropriate moment, share with the wife your conversations with the husband. Tell her of your interest in being of help in bringing the husband to a commitment to Jesus Christ. Ask if it would be possible to come by the home after they have had plenty of time to settle in with the new baby.

I think it is quite important to use the occasion of the arrival of the baby (the seriousness of thought which it provokes on the part of the mother and the father) to try to introduce a larger dimension to life than making money or getting promoted on the job. Jerry's attitude toward racing and other things would suggest that he has not yet grown up. Some of the ways in which Jerry expresses his ambitions makes him sound like a married teen-ager. If this is true, then underneath all the talk there is a great deal of uncertainty and a great deal of need to which Christ speaks. The gospel has many different aspects which speak to the needs of modern man. One aspect is forgiveness and one is hope in death. However, I think that the one which would speak best to Jerry would be that Christ comes into the life and gives meaning to everything that we are doing—our family, our job, our hobbies, and our relationships to other people.

Jerry can be won to Christ with love and patience and a genuine interest in him and his family.

Herschel H. Hobbs . . .

Jerry Hinson has come to a crisis in his life, the birth of his first child. In that crisis, none of his *values* lend him any support. He is like a rudderless ship, adrift on a tossing sea of concern. By contrast, his companion in the hospital waiting room is calm, made so by his spiritual faith.

It is evident that Jerry's sense of values is materialistic. All that he talks about is a better job, more money, and the things which money can buy. He even thinks of his baby in terms of an income tax deduction. Evidently, his mania for "speed" is at least a mild problem between him and his wife. He admits that as a child his home life was not a happy one. By his own words, Jerry admits that religion played practically no part in it.

And yet, he wants his baby to have a better home than he has had. "The best won't be too good for my baby." "There's so much I want for myself and my family."

In dealing with Jerry I would begin at this point. I would commend him for these worthwhile aims. But I would endeavor to show him that these could not be truly realized in terms of material things. His own unrest in this crisis is evidence that there is much to be desired in his own life.

I would point out to him that the *best* for his family should begin with a Christian father and husband. Because he had not had a Christian home, he admitted, "My home life was not too happy. I certainly hope to make a better one for my children." In this light I would endeavor to show Jerry that with the coming of his baby he was assuming new responsibilities. And the primary responsibility was to make a happy home for his wife and child. This means that they must come first even before his mania for racing. I assume that since his wife faced childbirth calmly she was a woman of faith. Therefore, I would dwell upon his obligation to join his faith with hers in providing the kind of home which he envisioned for his child.

Two things which Jerry said provide a means of approach at this point. In response to his companion's statement about faith as a foundation, he said, "Maybe that foundation part is my trouble." But then he added, "I could never become a believer."

I would agree with him that he needed a foundation

upon which to build his hopes and dreams for his family. I would endeavor to show him that the only abiding foundation is faith, not in some *thing* but in some *one*. I would point out that he was already a "believer" but a believer in the wrong things. He needs a faith in some One. I would point out that God wants for him and his family the same thing that he desires—the *best*. And that best is an undergirding faith in Jesus Christ who alone can provide it.

Then I would read to Jerry 1 Corinthians 3:11–15, with stress upon verse 11: "For other foundation can no man lay than that is laid, which is Jesus Christ." I would show him the abiding nature of a life based upon Christ, and the temporary nature of a life based upon material things. Because he questioned the reality of hell, I would endeavor to show him that the fact of an eternal failure would be hell itself. And that Jesus could save him from that, to say nothing about any other element involved in the idea of hell.

The other statement upon which I would dwell concerns his words, "A guy has to be on the right escalator, the right transportation to the top." To the top of what?

I would observe that material escalators could only take him to the top of material things. His present condition shows that material escalators are inadequate for the real needs of his life.

The *escalator* which he needs is Christ.

Therefore, I would read to him John 12:32: "And I, if I be lifted up from the earth, will draw all men unto me." I would explain what this means in terms of his sin and the death of Christ. And then by reading Acts 4:12, I would show that Christ is the only escalator: "Neither is there salvation in any other: for there is none other name under heaven given among men, whereby we must be saved."

I would then remind Jerry of his desires for his child and family, showing that their full realization must begin within himself. Assuming that I had his interest sufficiently, I would ask him to pray with me. I would pray for his wife in her delivery, for his child that it might be healthy, and for him that he would receive Jesus as his Saviour, that he and his wife through their mutual faith in Christ might lead their child to have a healthy spirit in a healthy body.

Thereafter, I would ask for a definite commitment from him. If he gave it, I would pray with him a prayer of thanksgiving. If he did not make a commitment, I would assure him of my continued prayers for him. I would ask him to promise to pray for himself, and arrange for another visit with him about the matter of the *best* for him and his family.

G. Avery Lee . . .

There are nine "John Smiths" in this book. Each is a distinct personality. Each is a person who needs the gospel. Some of the people may seem a bit unreal, but these are people I know, some of them quite well. There are traits of others which are wrapped up in several of these personalities. Naturally, I will read into these people some of my experiences with their counterparts.

There is a personal feeling that I do not have to succeed

in every case. That is, not every "John Smith" may come to a Christian decision. I am responsible for sowing the seed and seeing to its cultivation; someone else may be in on the harvest, if there is one, just as I have reaped where others have sown. This does not mean that I do not try in each case.

The reader will assume the use of Scripture searching, preaching, the plan of salvation, church attendance, consultation with others, and other procedures where possible, even if these are not specifically pointed out.

There is a deliberate avoiding of the old clichés, such as: soul-winning, personal witnessing, and the like. Such terms have no meaning to these "John Smiths," or to many who will work with them. My efforts will be directed more to bringing about a personal encounter with Jesus Christ, which issues in personal commitment, rather than in offering a set of propositions and asking for assent, or presenting a plan to be followed.

In discussing each case, a threefold formula will be used: *Diagnosis* of "John's" situation as it is described in the study; my *relationship* to him as a person; and an approach to find the right *prescription* which will get "John Smith" to take the gospel and find spiritual healing.

I am assuming the role of John (or Jane) Doe, Christian. That is, the person who introduces us to "John Smith."

Now a look at Jerry Hinson.

Diagnosis.—If the new friend in the hospital is representative, then the church doesn't have much chance with Jerry Hinson. Man, did that fellow ever botch it! Telling Jerry that he planned to succeed in business by being on the right escalator. How can a favorable response to the church be expected, unless Jerry figures that he and the new friend have the same set of materialistic values, and the church can be used as the right transportation to the desired goal? The church does not need any more such riders. Oh, he talks about faith, but the words have a hollow ring.

The birth of the first baby is one of the most anxiety-producing experiences in a man's life. Jerry's fright is pointed up in his reaction to the old-wives' tales. He is not consoled, even with support, because his own feelings are so strong. Perhaps these are guilt feelings because he goes to Daytona Beach and Indianapolis, taking his holidays apart from his wife.

It would help to know something about his wife. What is her attitude toward and relation with the church? What is her relationship with Jerry? Is his moonlighting a further excuse to get away from home, or is it from economic necessity?

Relationship.—Jerry's negative response toward the end is wrapped up in the fact that the friend has already revealed the hollowness of his own Christian experience. The friend is trying to get "all this world and heaven, too." He has just enough religion to make him a bore. He cannot leave it out, neither can he share it in a real, dynamic way.

If the new friend is to have any Christian influence at all, which is doubtful, there is a need to become acquainted on a broader, long-term basis. This hospital meeting is so chance and casual that little can come from such an encounter. Whether this kind of relationship can be established remains to be seen. Right now, it's all we have to go on, unless someone else is brought in.

Prescription.—Yes, you do get to know people pretty well on a trip, but the new friend missed the boat on this one. About the only thing he can do now is to be honest in saying, "Jerry, ol' buddy, I have a feeling that I muffed this one. I gave the impression that the church is a means to an end. Honest, Fellow, the church is more meaningful to me than that. Christian faith is really a part of my life, and I'd like another chance to tell you about it. What say we get together with our wives after they both get home and are up and about? Then we can get at this thing from a better angle. I promise not to try to sell you a bill of goods.

Unless such an approach is taken, where do we go from here? The only other avenue is if the faith of Jerry's wife is strong and significant enough to keep her in church. If she enrols the baby in the Cradle Roll, someone else may come on the scene. Jerry's desire to have everything just right for the baby just may be an approach—*if* the right person makes it. And this person probably is not the pastor, since Jerry has a built-in resentment of a "Holy Joe."

Editor's Note.—How would you witness to Jerry Hinson?

2

"I Just Don't Need What You've Got to Sell"

Jack D. Sanford

Frank Gammin is a hard-headed, young businessman who has made a tremendous success the hard way. He started a small business in our medium-sized city against the odds of discount houses and the large mass marketing techniques of the metropolitan center only an hour's drive away. He has fought the odds, and won a singular victory. His business is increasing yearly, and his reputation for quality and service have spread beyond our town.

But Frank Gammin is lost. He refuses to acknowledge his need for Christ, and insists that his family is also without need.

When I came to this town to be pastor of the Evergreen Church, I was told that Frank would not give me any trouble, but that I was wasting my time trying to interest him in the church. Of course, I have heard this before, but am constantly optimistic that just this once I will be able to overcome the past and win one of these die-hards to the Lord. But such has not been the case with Frank.

In my relationship with Frank, about all I have been able to do is gain a partial hearing once in a while. He never comes to church, but does seem to enjoy the time we spend occasionally over a cup of coffee at a little cafe near his place of business. Our conversation ranges the spectrum of male interests from the Baltimore Colts to the best possible time for the bass run at the local lake. However, every effort to engage him in creative discussion of his spiritual needs ends in failure. A typical example of his resistance to spiritual discussion is evident in the following conversation which we had only this past week. It went like this:

"Preacher, why are you always trying to get me saved? You think I'm some kind of king-sized devil?" Frank laughed as he sipped his coffee.

"No, Frank," I replied. "I don't think you're a king-sized devil. I just know you would be a better man if you were a Christian. And you'd have a much brighter future."

"Well," he drawled. "I don't see how being a Christian is going to help me. So, let's just enjoy our coffee without all this religion stuff," he suggested. "I like you, and I don't want to be rude to you. But Man, I just don't need what you've got to sell."

"Frank, there's not a man alive who doesn't need Christ, and that includes you." I had a strange feeling that my words had a hollow ring in the presence of such self-assurance.

"No, I don't need Christ," he continued. "I've got just about everything any man could possibly need. My family is well cared for, my business is going great, we have a summer cottage on the lake. Man, if I had anymore it'd kill me," he laughed.

"I must admit you've done exceptionally well these past

few years," I confessed. "But Frank, these are only material things you have. I'm talking about . . ."

"Yeah," he interrupted. "I know what you're driving at. You're trying to give me that spiritual stuff. I don't want any, thank you, 'cause I've had all the 'spiritual' nonsense I can take. It doesn't pay the bills, nor educate the kids, nor keep the wolf from the ol' door. No, I don't need that.

"I've seen it, Preacher. You see, my dad was spiritual. Yes sir," he continued sarcastically. "I can see him now, thanking the Lord for fatback meat, coarse cornbread, and beans, always beans. God, that's all we ever had at home. Half the time we were hungry, actually hungry, but Dad always put a little piece of money in the collection plate whenever it was passed around at the church. 'Little somethin' for the Lord,' he used to say. And for what? We stayed hungry and poor. Every nickel he gave to the church, Mom could have used a thousand times just to keep us warm and fed."

Frank stopped talking, and a hard glint came into his eyes.

"Besides," he began, "the kind of 'spiritual' junk I grew up with is for the birds. We were dragged off to church a half dozen times a week to hear a long-winded, ignorant preacher harangue us about the terrible sin of smoking cigarettes and going to the picture show. We were afraid to breathe, 'cause God might be hiding behind some bush, ready to pounce on us. I don't need that kind of stuff."

His tone was defiant and belligerent.

"Frank, I'm the last man in the world who would try to interest you in that kind of narrow emotionalism. What I would like you to see is the many wonderful things you are missing by being a stranger to a God of wonderful love. You have a great potential for good if only you would turn your life over to Christ."

I wanted to go on, to warn him about the future with all its uncertainties, to ask where he thought his strength would come from when some unexpected crisis swept down upon him. But the look on his face stopped me. He was dead serious, staring intently into my eyes, and I knew that he had something to say which he wanted me to hear.

"Preacher," he spoke slowly and deliberately. "I want us to get something straight, once and for all."

He looked me up and down, as though trying to determine whether or not he wanted to continue. Finally, he took a deep breath and continued.

"I hope what I have to say won't have any bad effect on our friendship. I like you and would like to continue to be your friend. I think you are an intelligent man, a good man, not an ignorant, long-winded preacher." He smiled to soften the tinge of bitterness which echoed his words.

"But please try to understand," he continued. "I don't need Christ, or God, or religion." He paused a moment, gazing out into the busy street. When he continued, the bitterness was still in his voice.

"When I was a boy, I had this stuff crammed down my throat morning and night, 'til I was so sick of religion I could have screamed. And nothing ever came of it . . . religion didn't do anything for us. Our family didn't get any better off financially, and they stayed backward and timid all their lives. They were always afraid they would do something wrong, and God would send them to hell.

Religion made them prisoners, and they just went through the motions of life.

"When I left home to serve with the Army in Korea, and then later, when I had the chance to go to college, I discovered a world neither I nor my family knew existed. It was a wonderful world. A real world where a man could become whatever his courage and strength were equal to. It was a place where courage and action were honorable, and set a man free. When I left home I discovered, for the first time, what it was to be free and alive in a real world.

"I liked that world, and I worked hard to get what I could out of it. Man, I really worked. And I saved every dime I could get my hands on. I took some risks, too, 'cause I wasn't afraid of anything. For instance, I went in debt over $50,000 for this business, and for months I worked like a dog just to keep my head above water. It was just me, grinding it out, day after day. Nobody was there to help me, Preacher, you understand that? Nobody! It was just me against all the odds. And I won!!

"Now it's all mine. I have a college education, a good family, a business which is debt free and making a nice profit each year, and my future is secure. All this is mine, and I'm still young enough to enjoy it. I'm happy, happy as a man could be.

"Besides all this, I live a good life. I mean the kind of life I lead is good. I'm not a drunk, or profane, nor would I ever cheat. You know the kind of man I am. You know how hard I've worked to gain the good reputation I have. And it is a good one. Folks around here will tell you, 'If Frank Gammin tells you somethin,' then you better believe it, 'cause he's a square shooter.' I'm proud of that, Preacher, and that's the way I live every day. It's the way I've always lived. I do right by people, and I'm just what I appear to be. And that's more than I can say about some of the phonies who make so much noise about religion.

"I knew some of those kind back home, and there are a few of them here in our town. They are the first ones at church every time the doors open, but, Man, you better watch them on Monday. They shortchange you, palm off second-class merchandise as if it were premium stuff, and lie like hell for a dollar. They're phony, that's all you can say about them.

"Well, I'm not like that. I'm honest, I work hard, I've made a success of my life. I got where I am without religion, and now—well, I just don't need what you have to sell."

HOW TO WIN THIS PERSON TO CHRIST
Kenneth L. Chafin . . .

Principle.—Those who succeed have just as much need for the hand of God in their lives as those who fail. It is true that the grace of God applies to people who make a miserable wreck of their lives. There are no circumstances in which a man can get himself that God cannot work with him to deal creatively and redemptively with his problems. However, the grace of God has just as much to say to the man who is succeeding. People who exercise power; people who have control over the lives of others; people who amass wealth; people who have great influence in the community—all desperately need to have God at work in their lives.

In thinking of all the people in all the different cases in this book, I probably react to this one more strongly than to any of the others. The real reason that I react to Frank Gammin the way I do is that I am offended by any person who has to brag on himself. I do not believe that any reflective person is ever quite as satisfied with his life as this man sounds. I know too many people who are rich and powerful, but do not find fulfilment in these things. I do not believe that he is as well off as he pretends.

You will recall that at one time Jesus was confronted with a man who had done so well that his conversation with himself had to do with all his goods. He decided that he was going to eat, drink, and be merry because he had enough to last him all his life. You also recall that Jesus called the man a fool. (See Luke 12:20). I think that what bothers me most about Frank is that he is made in the image of God, yet he persists in interpreting the meaning of life on a very materialistic plane.

The world is full of Frank Gammins. One time I went with an older minister to visit a man very much like Frank. I began my conversation by saying, "I know you are one of the finest men in our community and you are highly thought of by everyone." The older minister with whom I was visiting interrupted me and said, "I am sure that Kenneth is sincere in all that he says, but I don't believe it. If you have lived as many years as I have in this world and you have had the temptations that I have, on the outside you may appear to be a very good man, but on the inside you know you are not good."

The man dropped his head and was very quiet for a minute. Then he looked up with tears in his eyes and said to the older minister, "You're right." I wondered what he had thought about all those ministers who had come out and patted him on the back for being such a great guy when he knew what his thoughts were and what his motives were. While this may not be a good method, it illustrated to me a profound truth, "There is none righteous, no, not one" (Rom. 3:10).

One approach to Frank might be to ask a couple of people who are actually more "successful" than he is but who have found a meaningful relationship with Jesus Christ to go see him. At least they would get through to him the fact that they have everything that he has, and much more!

I would also try to get acquainted with his wife and children and try to speak to his own spiritual needs through them. Oftentimes, a man sounds like the Chamber of Commerce in his business and yet, in his relationship to his family he has the same sense of inadequacies as anyone else. This might be a starting place to touch him for God.

I think that it might be good to try to discuss what it means to be a Christian in some terminology other than the traditional "lost-and-saved" language. It is obvious that Frank has such a stereotype of this terminology that he doesn't really understand what the minister is saying. It may be that Frank has been asking himself some very religious questions in some nonchurch terminology. Becoming sensitive to this might be a part of winning him.

Herschel H. Hobbs . . .

Brother! Jack Sanford has certainly come up with one! And yet is Frank so singular? Unfortunately, the woods are full of them, only most of them are not as forthright as Frank Gammin. Compared to Frank, the *down-and-outs* are a picnic. Surely the Frank Gammins can be won. But how?

Frank is a self-made, self-confident, self-righteous man. He may not be a "king-sized devil," but the devil has him anyway, held in the clutches of material success but with no sense of a spiritual need.

Frank belittles the spiritual training of his childhood home. I grant that the preaching which he heard may not have been conducive to a proper understanding of God as love, but I wonder if he has not credited himself with values which he received in this sort of religious environment.

He boasts of honesty, character, and industriousness. Where did he get these things? Not in Korea or in the business jungle. I think I would try to show him that these things came out of the childhood environment which he now despises.

And is it true that "nobody" helped him? What about the banker, his customers, his employees, and his community? He is not as much a self-made man as he thinks. But more. What about God? Why was Frank not killed in Korea? Whence came his health, his life, his mental and spiritual strength? Yes, his children? But how can Frank be led to see this?

Well, I think that after his tirade, I would ask for the same courtesy that I had extended to him. I would ask him to hear me out as I presented to him the plan of salvation. I would appeal to him as a self-admitted fair man to do so. Then I would give him all that I have, pulling no punches.

To begin with, I would assure Frank that God loves him in spite of his attitude. Then I would remind him of the source of his moral character. I would point out God's blessings upon him. But I would certainly show how limited these things are to bear him up in a crisis.

Then I would read to him and explain the story of the rich young ruler. (See Luke 18:18–23.) I would show him that with *everything* he still lacked the most important thing, eternal life. I would tell Frank that Christ does not ask him to take a pauper's oath but to dedicate his things to God in service to man. I would show him straight from the shoulder that material things stand between him and God, and thus are his idols. And this makes him a pagan.

I would read to him Romans 2:4–6: "Or despiseth thou the riches of his goodness and forbearance and longsuffering; not knowing that the goodness of God bringeth thee to repentance? But after thy hardness and impenitent heart treasurest up unto thyself wrath against the day of wrath and revelation of the righteous judgment of God; who will render to every man according to his deeds." Yes, I would include some "hell," but show that Jesus out of love and mercy warned us against it.

Frank thinks that he is not a "king-sized devil." So I would read to him John 3:16. Then I would read and explain John 3:18: "He that believeth on him is not condemned: but he that believeth not is condemned already, because he hath not believed in the name of the only begotten Son of God." I would show him that the greatest sin is not cheating in business but refusing to believe in Jesus as his Saviour. It is to accuse God of the murder of his own Son—if such as Frank Gammin do not need to be saved.

I would then tell Frank how he could believe in Jesus—through trust and commitment of his life to him. then I would pray in Frank's presence, asking that God's Holy Spirit would break his heart and stubborn will.

Perhaps this would not win him immediately—maybe never, but I would deliver my soul by witnessing to him. Then I would continue to drink coffee with him or do any other proper thing to stay close to him. It may take some tragedy in Frank's life to shake him out of his complacency. But if it should come, I would be on hand to help and to guide him into a saving experience with Christ.

G. Avery Lee . . .

Diagnosis.—It is obvious that Frank Gammin *does* have a god, perhaps two—material success and basic integrity. It is a "self-made man" image that he worships. Can he make room for a God who will put these other gods in proper perspective?

Frank's "I was forced as a child" is a cover-up, but we do not yet know what this "insecure-secure" man is hiding. If that early church held out a "brighter future," we can understand his resentment of a church getting money when a lad needed food for present hunger. (I know a preacher who must have a year's supply of food in his deep freeze for the same reason—a power failure would crush him! And a doctor who must have fifty pairs of shoes in his closet because as a boy he had to stuff newspapers in his shoes.)

Although he rejects old-time emotionalism, there seems to be no intellectual difficulties. Is there a hidden moral one? Frank is evidently a good family man. What about his wife? Is she a Christian? Active or inactive? Does she badger him about the church? Does she want to give money to the church?

Frank has little regard for preachers, especially the present pastor's predecessors. They pressed him so incessantly that he is further alienated. Despite Frank's professed friendship, the present pastor had better take it easy.

Frank is not going to be scared into heaven with threats of hell. Korea demonstrated that even a fox hole religion is not for him. There is a chink in his armor someplace. A future crisis will reveal the weakness and he will need assistance.

Relationship.—I like Frank Gammin and appreciate his honesty. I would prefer him to level with me instead of using that bit about his father. One of these days I'll hit him with, "Come on, Frank, what's really bugging you?" Why can't I be honest with him and accept him as he is? In saying, "I just know you'd be a better man," I really say, "You're not acceptable as you are." This creates instant hostility, and Frank bristles, "I don't need what you've got to sell." I ask Christ to accept me as I am; so Frank must be accepted. Later, he'll find the something better.

In one of his sermons, Harry Emerson Fosdick has said that every island has its "near side," the one right place where a landing is made. He has also said that every man has his near side, too, where the gospel can get in. I am to keep alert and available so as to see it when it appears in Frank.

Friendship will keep the communication lines open so that when the crisis appears, I, or someone else, can get in. So, I'll keep drinking coffee with him, talk about the Baltimore Colts, and go fishing. Religion, the church, the necessity of salvation do not have to intrude on every conversation.

Prescription.—Slow and easy is the best approach to

Frank. Liking me, he'll not object when I come around, if a text from the Scriptures is not "crammed down his throat."

Perhaps there is a Fellowship of Christian Athletes at the local school. The coach may be a Christian. At some rally a member of the Baltimore Colts, or some other athletic whom he respects, could be invited as speaker and Frank could come along.

Frank's attitude toward businessmen who are Christian is unfortunate. Not all of them are the hypocrites he thinks they are. If I could find one man whom he respects, that man would be of much help.

Frank needs to know that I like him, respect him, and am interested in him as a person. He knows what I represent. Therefore, I need to keep the lines open and be available when he is ready and needs help.

Editor's Note.—How would you witness to this person?

3

"All This Repentance Stuff Is Not for Me"

William L. Self

Jeff Franklin is an exceptionally handsome man in his late forties. Dressing in the height of fashion and looking the part of a middle-aged business tycoon, he leads what most Americans would call an exceptionally good life. He resides in one of the finest suburbs, has more than an adequate income, and can afford to participate in the most exclusive and expensive recreational endeavors. Jeff has an attractive wife and two children. He is surrounded by a covey of efficient, adoring secretaries and junior executives. For them, his wish is their command.

Jeff's success in his business, professional, and community life has not been followed by success in his personal and family life. He senses a deep longing within for something more than the fruits of a good life. He knows that he cannot live by bread alone but objects to any alternative. He is too proud to admit the need for salvation, but his inner hurting demands some kind of answers.

One day, in response to his call, I was ushered to a place in a comfortable chair in a deeply carpeted office—the kind of office which is the essence of success, authority, and position. Jeff did not spar around with me. He came right to the point and said: "Look, Bill, we're both busy men. Let me put it to you this way. My family and I are looking for a church. What does yours have to offer?"

The conversation ran on something like this:

"We have the normal activities that any suburban church would have. Tell me something about your family."

"Well, you know we have a boy in high school and a girl in junior high. We've been married for twenty-five years. Immediately after World War II, I broke into this business and it's been very good for me. I got in on the ground floor and came up with the company. I've worked all the way up. As you know, I live on the North Side in the finest section of town. Our children attend the finest schools. We live and eat well and have everything life could give us."

"Why do you want a church?"

"Well, my wife and I were talking about that the other night. It suddenly occurred to us that, although the children are getting some size on them now, we're bringing them up without any religious teachings. Now, I don't want all this hellfire-and-brimstone, repentance, sin, and salvation stuff. A man does have to have something to believe."

"What's your religious background?"

"My family traveled a lot; so we never really got involved in any one denomination. However, in the Service I always told them I was a Protestant, simply because I was sure I wasn't Roman Catholic. My wife has about the same story. She likes the Methodist Church near our house but would be willing to go anywhere with me. We're sort of looking around."

"Are there any other reasons why you suddenly feel the need for some type of religious expression?"

"No, not really. We have the usual problems at home that any family has. Let's quit sparring around. I'll level with you straight. Our high-school boy is in a state of complete rebellion, laughs at what he calls our 'middle-class values,' won't do anything we say, demands the car all the time, and has been in trouble with the police. If things continue as they are, he'll not graduate from high school. We also suspect that he's had more than a casual relationship with the young lady he is dating. We just really haven't given him much except food, clothing, and shelter while he was growing up."

"I see. Is there anything else I should know about the family? How do you and your wife get along?"

"Why do you ask?"

"I was really trying to see whether you were united in this or whether this was just your idea."

"Well, we're not united in much of anything. We haven't had much of a marriage for the last ten years. It has degenerated into sort of a tired friendship. I told her the other day that I felt as if I lived in a $1,500-a-month boarding house."

"What do you mean?"

"The first of every month I give her a check for $1,500 with which to run the house, and I come and go as I please. I spent last weekend in Puerto Rico, and week after next I'm flying to Washington to watch the Falcons play the Redskins. After that, I'll go on up to New York for a convention with some friends. She has her life; I have mine. But there's very little communication between us."

"How does she feel about all this?"

"She doesn't like it. She'd like for me to come home at five o'clock every evening and work in the garden. She doesn't care about football and when I stay home in the evening, there's not very much to talk about. We fuss about money, the children, and life in general. She doesn't like my friends and I don't like hers. She spends her time as an amateur psychiatrist, trying to work me over and lets me know frankly that I'm juvenile, insecure, and not meeting her needs. So far as I'm concerned, I'm providing pretty well for my family even though I'm 'juvenile and insecure.' She doesn't mind the money I give her. She has unlimited credit at all the big stores in the city and does what she pleases."

"How did the church get involved in all this?"

"We can't go on like we are. The other night we had a long talk. We talked about Jeff Jr.'s problems. The only real solution which we could find to the whole thing was perhaps to go to church."

"Where have you attended?"

"Nowhere, yet. As I said, I was out of town last week. Every time the Falcons are in town, I give a brunch on Sunday morning for my friends and then we all go to the game."

"What you're actually saying to me is that you're hoping that somehow a relationship with the church can unravel some of your personal and domestic problems."

"I guess that's right. Do you or your church have anything for me?"

The conversation continued. He agreed that we'd meet again but that he and his family wanted to attend our church.

A few weeks later, I went back to Jeff's office and we talked again at length. His family had not attended our church in the meantime and in a moment of real honesty, he turned and began the conversation:

"I guess I'd really better level with you. The other day when you were in my office, I didn't tell you the whole story. One of the real problems which my wife and I fuss over is that I just haven't been as loyal to her as I should have been the last few years."

"Tell me what you mean."

At this point he went into a detailed discussion of some indiscretions that he had had on his frequent weekend trips. No lasting relationships outside the home had been established, but casual contacts had produced a real division in his home. Then there was a lengthy discussion on his part, justifying his actions because of his own insecurity and the inadequacy of his own home.

When he finished this, I simply said to him: "I believe your problem is not so much establishing a relationship with the church, although this will come, but rather it's the need to know Jesus Christ as your Saviour. Frankly, we're not interested in reform. We're interested in repentance and conversion."

"You mean to tell me that before I can be a member of your church, I'm going to have to say I'm a sinner and repent just like children do?"

"Precisely, for you see the basic thing our church members have in common is that we're a band of sinners who have repented."

"Frankly, I'm not willing to come in on this basis. Church membership—yes, but all this repentance, sin, and salvation stuff is not for me. I like you personally, but I surely didn't think that a church in this day would require its members to publicly declare their sinfulness. I'm just not ready to do this yet. My problems are emotional, psychological, and the fact that my wife is unsympathetic. I'll just have to work them out myself."

This was not our last conversation, but conversations that followed from this point on did not go much further. Later conversations were still on the surface. To my knowledge Jeff's personal situation has not changed one bit and probably has degenerated some. Jeff Franklin is still a successful, affluent, powerful, handsome sinner.

HOW TO WIN THIS PERSON TO CHRIST
Kenneth L. Chafin . . .

Principle.—There are truths an individual cannot get across which a group, like the church, can. The church can bear a composite witness to a person or a family.

On the surface, Jeff Franklin sounds like everyone's ideal. The first three paragraphs describing Jeff give the impression that he has "arrived."

It is difficult to assess a person's motive and seldom wise. A person's first reaction is that Jeff is discussing his spiritual problems because his teen-ager is in trouble and because he is having difficulty with his wife. All any of us have to do is to look into our own lives to realize that God uses many experiences and many types of relationships to speak his word to us. I would think that the Holy Spirit has probably been using Jeff's sense of frustration, his relationship to his wife, and his relationship to his children to speak to him about his own spiritual needs.

In all likelihood, Jeff would have such a caricature in his mind of what repentance and conversion really means that the pastor may not really have communicated to him what he was talking about. Some of the most familiar words have fuzzy meaning to many individuals.

It is pretty obvious that everyone in the Franklin family needs not only the kind of salvation that puts a person into a right relationship with God, but the kind of salvation that allows individuals to live in a right relationship with one another. God not only saves individuals, but he can save marriages and relationships between parents and children. The only source of forgiveness is God, and God is able not only to forgive our sins but to help us to forgive one another the sins that we commit against each other. I would see that the only hope for this man to be a truly successful man in all of his relationships is to come to know God in this kind of relationship.

The fact that the man has "cooled off" and is not willing to discuss further his needs ought not to be interpreted as meaning he is not interested. In all likelihood, he was somewhat embarrassed that he shared a matter of such importance and has withdrawn. This does not mean that he has now come to feel that he is completely satisfied with this. It is a strange phenomenon in today's world but very often we can speak most glibly about what is least important, and we speak with more reticence about what is of greatest importance.

Make an effort to talk with the couple, together at their home. I do not think that the best place would be at the place of business.

I would be tempted to make a proposition to them and to make a couple of requests of them. *First,* ask them to make a break with the pattern of living which they have become stuck in for a certain period of time. This would involve her spending more time with him and his spending more time at home.

Second, ask them both, with their children, to expose themselves consistently during this period to the church, its fellowship, and its worship.

This marriage and these lives did not get this way overnight. There are so many forces in a secular world to raise seriously the question of the possibility of living any other way. Unless they can get to the church and can discover in the church's worship and in its fellowship some spiritual resources, they will not even have faith to believe that they can start over with God and can start over with one another. I have been absolutely amazed at the redeeming and therapeutic quality of a worshiping community. I would make a major effort to get this family related with some of the church's life.

Herschel H. Hobbs . . .

In the eyes of the world Jeff Franklin *has it made.* But in his own eyes he is a failure. He has failed as a husband and father. Neither he nor his wife are Christians. In their selfish interests they have little home life. And Jeff sees its bitter fruit being borne in his son's life. It is evident that he is under conviction of the Holy Spirit but too proud to admit the need for salvation. He inquires about a church when his need is the Saviour. He wants religious teachings for his children, but teachings which he prescribes in advance. In fact, this is his whole trouble. From Jeff's position of power, he is accustomed to giving orders, not taking them. Even now he wants to lay down his terms to God. He is unwilling to admit that he is a sinner in need of a Saviour. Even in his "indiscretions," he seeks to justify his actions. Everybody is at fault but Jeff.

Of course, it is obvious that Jeff Franklin is "a successful, affluent, powerful, handsome sinner." But how can I show him that this is true?

I think that in dealing with Jeff Franklin I would use Jesus' interview with Nicodemus. Of course, not every detail is parallel, certainly not with respect to Jeff's "indiscretions." But basically, the problem is the same—an outwardly affluent man with a deep inward need.

I would take Nicodemus as an example of a man who in the eyes of the world *had it made*—position, power, perhaps wealth, influence, yes, and character. I would point out the parallels in Jeff's life. But I would also point out his sins.

Then I would show how that, in spite of his position, Nicodemus felt a lack in his life. Evidently, it was this lack which caused him to seek out Jesus. But I would show that the last thing which Nicodemus expected was to hear that he needed an inner change. I would then apply this to Jeff's own attitude. He wanted only to join a church as he would a club, giving no place to the spiritual elements involved.

Then I would show the demand which Jesus made upon Nicodemus. "Except a man be born again, he cannot see the kingdom of God" (John 3:3). I would point out what a shock this was to Nicodemus, much like the shock Jeff received at the idea of confessing his sins. Nicodemus wanted to converse about the kingdom of God, yet he was not even in it. Applying Jesus' teachings, I would show how Jeff wanted to join a church without even qualifying to be part of the church of Jesus Christ.

Then I would seek to explain what Jesus meant by being born again or from above. Like Nicodemus, Jeff had been born naturally into a natural family relationship, and in that relationship had reached certain attainments. But if he wanted to be a child of God he must be born spiritually into spiritual relationships. And with God's help, he could achieve in the spiritual sphere as he had done in the natural sphere.

Jeff objected to saying, "I'm a sinner and repent just like children do." I would show him that such a decision is exactly what Jesus demands. (See Matt. 18:3). Then from this Scripture verse, I would contrast the natural and spiritual births. I would endeavor to show him the mystery of being born of the Spirit. Pointing out that his unrest was due to the conviction of the Holy Spirit, I would seek to show Jeff that he must permit the Holy Spirit to lead him further to repentance and faith in Jesus Christ.

At this point I would remind him that he could not merely *reform* his problems. He must begin all over by giving his children a Christian father. His empty homelife and "indiscretions" were due to the fact that he and his wife had nothing in common. They must find a center of life through a mutual faith in Jesus Christ.

I would then read to Jeff John 3:16. I would point out that God loves him and has a plan for his life. But because of his sin of unbelief toward Christ, the greatest of sins, he had not availed himself of God's love and purpose. But God has shown his love to him in his Son. I would point out what the Son has done to save him and to make possible God's plan for him. I would explain to Jeff that "everlasting life" is something that he receives now. It is the quality of life which is now and which abides in eternity.

I would tell him that this life can be his through faith in

Jesus Christ. Because it is a mystery, we must receive it by faith, not through understanding. I would explain that faith is both trust and commitment. Trust in Christ as Saviour and a life committed to his care and service.

Having done these things I would then try to bring Jeff to a decision. I would pray, and then ask him to pray. I would ask him to humble himself before God as a little child, confess his sins, and ask for forgiveness. I would ask him to pray, "God be merciful to me a sinner" (Luke 18:13). If he did, then I would ask him to place his hand in mine as evidence that he was trusting in Jesus as his Saviour.

Assuming that he did so, then I would pray with Jeff a prayer of thanksgiving. I would request the privilege of talking with his wife and children about their need for Christ. Then I would endeavor to lead all who receive him to make a public profession of faith and to receive baptism into the fellowship of the church.

G. Avery Lee . . .

Diagnosis.—Here is a man who is hurting all over—the ulcer type: hard on the outside, soft on the inside. The outer facade of success is being eaten away with failure. This is a family affair. Neither he nor his wife want to continue as they are. While enjoying the affluent life, they recognize something is missing. Give him credit for believing that the church can supply the missing ingredient. He is looking for a place to put his dependency, something to stop his manipulative power so that he can again relate to people. We have a good bit going for us. Let's not botch it with the wrong approach.

As a man of action, surrounded by those whose command is his wish, Jeff Franklin wants his problems solved . . . yesterday! It has taken a long time to tie himself and his family in these knots. They will not unravel all at once. Some knots may never come untied, even if he "gets saved and joins the church."

Relationship.—Above all else, Jeff Franklin needs to know that he can trust me. Listening to him as he opens up, I must not allow him to overexpose himself. He needs to know that I can respect him, accept him as he is, and love him. It is not enough for him to feel respected; he needs to be accepted and loved for himself. He said that the reasons for his indiscretions are his insecurity, his need to be loved, and his inadequacy at home. The same lack is obvious in his wife, his son, and will be in his daughter, perhaps more so.

There will be a need for me to avoid any trace of envy of his success and affluence. I cannot be the TV station flunky. I must be the pastor. Jeff may take a notion to "do things" for me—take me on trips, to ball games, or give me a personally tailored suit in an effort to buy his way in. He must realize that I am shepherd of the flock, not his pet lamb. *So must I!* Much as the church needs the Jeff Franklins, there can be no favoritism in this "courtship." He wouldn't respect the church if he suspected that.

My attitude must be one of patience, not expecting him or the family to solve everything at once. Some of this same patience must rub off on him.

Prescription.—I would never have said to Jeff Franklin, "Frankly, we're not interested in reformation. We're interested in repentance and conversion." Why alienate him at the very beginning? Why not be interested in his reformation? That is what he needs and wants. Reformation is a part of repentance or it had better be! Which comes first is immaterial. True, Jeff needs to be confronted with his sin and need of Christ as Saviour. He has already acknowledged this in terms he understands. It is hard for "Mr. Big" to apply the term "sinner" to himself, but he will . . . if! If he can see himself accepting God's grace as something he cannot buy, as he buys everything else.

Jeff needs some things outside the church. He can't cut off all his friends, nor can his wife. He could go home occasionally and putter in the garden. Does Junior play ball at school, or in the band? Has Jeff ever seen him play? Has he ever shown Junior the inner workings of television?

Get the Franklin family coming to church, even on the reformation basis. Get them interested in something outside themselves where they can give instead of get. Other things will fall in place as we go along. Getting started is the thing.

Kindly pastoral care will determine if professional counseling is needed; just so the pastor holds on to him. Stable, pastoral care will undergird Jeff while the kinks are being straightened out. There is no need for him to hurt when help is available.

EDITOR'S NOTE.—How would you witness to Jeff Franklin?

4

Forget About the Money-grabbing Churches

Harold E. Dye

Beside the curving sidewalk leading to the tree-shaded brick house, a wrought iron sign swinging from a column of fieldstone announced simply: *The Hefleys.*

Immaculate, thick, green lawns flowed out from either edge of the sidewalk, swirling now and then about the boles of shaggy, giant oaks, finally to terminate at white picket fences shutting the modest estate from the rest of the world.

It was exactly the kind of place one would expect the retired owner of the Chevrolet Agency to call home. The former boss of one of the towns' leading business enterprises could not be happy in a crackerbox tract house—not old Tom Hefley who once fired his best mechanic for getting grease on the steering wheel of an "uppity" lady customer's Impala.

Tom, himself, could be seen squatting in a pair of snow-white coveralls, working a trowel into a bed of roses up near the porch of the house.

The little Volkswagen slid to a stop near the swinging sign and its driver turned to his companion, and said,

"There's the old boy now, out in the rose bed. He doesn't look so vicious, does he?"

"No," answered the other nervously, "He looks harmless enough. It's not that I am afraid of him. Why should I be? It is just that I am afraid of failure. I don't know what to say, nor even how to act. And I *am* afraid of me—afraid that Hefley might say something to trigger my cussed temper and I would rip into him before I could think. After all, he is a pretty sharp-tongued character. . . ."

"I don't know what to say, either," admitted the driver. Suddenly they were no longer middle-aged church men, but little boys, helpless and afraid.

The man nearest the curb placed his hand on the door handle but paused as the other said quietly, "We are going in there to represent God; let's ask him to go with us."

The prayers were short, hardly a sentence each, but both men felt better afterwards. They passed through the stone gate with its wrought iron sign and walked confidently toward the house. As they drew near, the man in the white coveralls stood stiffly to his feet. His bones creaked, and he smiled ruefully.

"Just a fugitive from Medicare," he said. "Why, it's Bill Stevens and Jim Haywood. Glad to see you. Don't tell me both of you overgrown peckerwoods rode that poor little beetle over here!" He nodded toward the little car down by the gate.

Bill laughed. "That Volkswagen may not get there as fast as a Chevy, but it sure gets there cheaper. Jim and I came out to talk with you a few minutes, if you have the time."

"Time! That I've got. Oodles and gobs of time. I sure made a mistake retiring right in the prime of life. I'd a whole lot rather smell the bright clean smell of a brand new car than to smell the scent of roses, with due apologies to the Almighty. Come in! Jane'll fix you a pot of java, but I warn you it won't be fit to drink. That woman makes coffee as weak as a . . . as a . . Volkswagen's compression. Haw haw! Hey, Jane! Company!"

A trim little woman came to the door, wiping her hands on a spotless apron. "Come in, come in," she invited, and her eyes were almost misty. Jane Hefley knew why the men from First Baptist were there. She had been praying for just such a visit for a long, long time. She covered her interest carefully. "Tom doesn't like coffee. He drinks concentrated lye. It's enough to burn out the lining of his stomach."

"Get along with you, Woman," her husband said cheerfully, "and throw in an extra handful of coffee. Grab yourselves a couple of chairs," he said to his visitors.

The two men felt relieved. This was not bad. Maybe old Tom had mellowed in retirement. Anyway, so far, so good.

"Now, is there any special reason you boys strained the innards of that beetle by making it bring you out here—especially since it is Saturday and the bass are taking jitterbugs on Miller Lake?"

"A very special reason, Tom," said Bill Stevens softly, "You. We came to tell you about the most wonderful thing which has happened to us in our whole lives—our salvation through Christ, and to see if you can find him, too. We are interested in you, Tom, and we want the happiness which we know to be yours as well."

A gradual change had come over the face of their host. The lines around his mouth hardened and his eyes grew bleak.

"You are wasting your time," he said shortly. "In the first place, I take issue with your statement about happiness. I have an idea that I am much happier than either of you is at this very moment. I don't think I have missed a thing in not being a Christian. At least I am my own boss and I don't feel any compulsion to go about meddling in my neighbor's personal affairs. I let him live his own life, and no so-called Holy Spirit sends *me* out on a wild goose chase like you are on right now. Sure, I'll admit that it might give you a small feeling of satisfaction to go back to the brethren with my scalp tied to your belt, but I am about to deny you the privilege. I don't mean to be rude, fellows, but that's just the way it is."

"Tom," said Bill gently, "we didn't come here to argue with you, but to relate our own experiences with Christ and to let you see what he has done for us."

"And in the second place," said their host, ignoring the words of his guest, "all of these years I have gotten along without the church. Frankly, I never missed that, either. I have worked hard all of my life, including Sundays. When do you suppose your church people go looking for automobiles to buy? I'll tell you: Sunday. When do they fill up their tanks with gas? Sunday. I couldn't afford to close up shop completely on Sunday. As I said, I have worked hard all of my life. That is my religion—work. And it has paid off. I have this nice home, a comfortable income from stocks and bonds, and don't owe any man anything. Here's our java. Thank you, Honey."

Mrs. Hefley extended white china cups on a silver platter, with cream and sugar shimmering in silver vessels. She served her husband last. "Be nice," she admonished, and there was wistfulness in her voice. She returned to the kitchen.

"There goes the queen of all the earth. I give her all the love you want me to give to God. At least she is alive to take it. You know, I almost lost her a year ago. . . ."

"We know." Jim Haywood spoke for the first time. "We prayed for her at church. Our pastor was right by her side during the crisis. . . ."

"I know, I know," was the gruff reply, "and I appreciate all that. Believe me, I do. I know the church was interested in her. As for the preacher of the church, I know he was there. It is his business. It's what he gets paid to do. And my Jane has always done her part financially. I give her five dollars every week of the world to stick in the collection plate when it is shoved under her nose on Sunday. But if, as you say, God healed her, why did I have to dig up three thousand dollars for the doctor and the hospital?" The last was said low so that his wife, busy in the kitchen, could not hear.

Haywood fought down a sharp reply. His cheeks flushed with sudden anger and he looked away, not trusting himself to speak.

"I've got my reasons for not liking the church," Tom went on. "I was about to join it once just to please Jane. Then I got my eyes opened. Do you know how? I was just starting in business. A good deacon traded me a 1925 Buick. 'That car is mechanically perfect,' he said and had me listen to it run. It purred like a kitten at a bowl of milk.

I sold it to a farmer and he drove it twenty miles and the main bearings went out. Believe it or not those mains had been replaced with leather. That's what I said, *Leather*. That made it run quiet enough to sell to me. I said right then and there I would never have anything to do with a church as long as I lived. And I won't . . . personally. I knew a preacher once. . . ."

"Tom," Bill Carter said patiently. He got no further.

"All right, all right! I won't tell about the preacher, or the passel of others who were good church members but who would cheat you out of your eyeballs. I live by the Golden Rule, myself, and if that is not enough to get me to heaven, I don't know what is. That doesn't say anything about getting yourself baptized and into a church and giving a tenth of all that you make to the preacher."

Jim Haywood spoke. "Tom, do you believe in God?"

"Of course, I believe in God. Do you think I am a confounded heathen? Anybody has to believe in God if he has any sense at all. And," a look of cunning came into the gray eyes, "you both admit that Christ is God, so if I say I believe in God that makes me believe in Christ according to your own notion, and if I believe in Christ, Jane says I will get to heaven. And I still don't have to join any church and pay the 10 percent of my income to the preacher." There was a note of triumph in his voice.

"But Tom, the Bible indicates right here. . . ."

"I've read it, whatever it is you are wanting to show me. But I'll tell you one thing. Nowhere in that Bible do I read that you have to join the church to be saved."

"Of course you haven't," said Bill in exasperation, "But it does say. . . ."

"Look, fellows, we have been friends a long time, right? I appreciate you coming out to see me, especially since I have made a lot of noise about how I would throw anybody out of the house who came peddling that religion stuff. I know you mean well, but I am not buyin'. Now, why don't we just forget about the money-grabbin' churches and talk about something else? That way we can keep on being friends." There was steel in Tom's words.

Back at the little Volkswagen, Jim Haywood said, "How can you deal with a bird like that? What can you say?"

"Well, we tried. You know the old saying: 'You can lead a horse to water but you can't make him drink.' "

"Not if you muddy up the water. That's what worries me. Maybe *we* muddied the water. Let's tell the preacher all about it, and maybe he can show us where we went wrong, *if* we did."

HOW TO WIN THIS PERSON TO CHRIST
Kenneth L. Chafin . . .

Principle.—You will never meet a person who does not need Jesus Christ.

When the rich young ruler came to Christ, he brought everything Tom Hefley has plus a high view of Christ and religion. Yet, Jesus said to him, "One thing thou lackest" (Mark 10:21). No man is a success who defines life completely in getting goods.

I suppose that every person who has ever made an honest effort in witnessing has met the equivalent of Tom Hefley. I personally identify with the sense of inadequacy which characterize the men as they approached him and the sense of futility that seems to characterize them after the encounter which was described so well by Harold Dye.

Tom Hefley is the type of person who is described by people in the community as "a man who would give you the shirt off his back." I have some real doubts about this sort of man. First, although he professes to be a follower of the Golden Rule, I doubt seriously if he treated his two visitors as he would like to be treated by one of his prospective customers. I sense a type of emotional reaction that is not entirely consistent with people who feel secure in their unbelief.

Second, I doubt seriously if his reputation as a businessman is as lily white as he would lead one to believe by his criticism of the church. His argument about having to keep his business open on Sunday to serve the church members won't hold water. Most reputable new car dealers do not open their business on Sundays.

Third, I have a feeling that what he said does not represent what he actually feels down deep in his heart. This is a fairly standard reaction which he has worked up to religious people and which he has found quite successful in times past. He has embellished it in the using of it, but I doubt seriously if he feels any better after such an encounter.

Some effort needs to be made to get back behind what I would consider to be a fairly standard and fairly superficial response in an effort to discover what has been the religious pilgrimage of this person. I would suspect that he didn't share with these two men any of the real problems that he has, but that the problems go back much farther. The next time around it would be good to ask Tom some questions which would get him to talking about his early years and his parents' attitudes toward the church and his early contacts with the church. The problem probably lies somewhere in this area.

As a young man, I once went to visit a very rough man who was the head of a trucking industry. He had such a violent attitude toward the church that when his employees saw me come in they all left. After he had made a few noises about the church and was fairly certain that everyone was out of earshot he said to me in a very quiet voice, "Son, I am actually not as mean as I pretend and I am not as satisfied with my life as most people think. My problem is I'm just not sure I could be the kind of Christian God would want me to be and stay in this business." This was an example of a person who kept a very rough and rebellious exterior to cover up a very genuine sense of need that he was almost embarrassed to admit.

When a person has gone all the way through life with one set of standards and one set of values and one goal and this goal has not included God, this person is not going to give up without a struggle.

We all need to be aware of our personal inadequacies and of the fact that ultimately a Christian is a witness to the power of God in the life of an individual. I like the fact that the men stopped and in prayer acknowledged their dependence upon God in their witness.

The fact that two men from the church took time out to come and sit down and be insulted by this man may in the long run be used of God as effectively as anything they said. I think there are certain ways in which we witness, simply by allowing ourselves to be exposed to what other people think about us and still expressing an interest and concern for them. Whether there were obvious results or not, God will bless the praying wife and the interested friends.

Herschel H. Hobbs . . .

"Pastor, you've heard our story. Evidently we failed. And we want you to tell us where we went wrong."

"Well, fellows, in the first place, you haven't failed. You have witnessed to a lost man. And that is never a failure. If anybody has failed it is Tom Hefley. He failed to respond favorably to the witness of two concerned friends.

"Now as to where you 'went wrong,' that's another matter. Any of us can always look back and see where he might have done differently.

"In the first place, you didn't go wrong in being afraid before going to Tom's home. I'm always afraid when I go to talk to a lost person. To witness for Christ is a great responsibility. Of course, there are many people like Tom. And we may be afraid of them. But I have a feeling that Tom isn't as sure of himself as he would have us to think. He is afraid to consider this matter seriously. So he tries to scare people off. But even though you were afraid, you did go to see him. And that's the very essence of courage.

"In the second place, you did right in praying about it before you went in the yard. None of us should ever try to win someone to Christ without first praying about it.

"But now, what about the case itself? As I listened to you I caught three very significant things. Tom spoke about cheating Medicare and how well off he is economically. I think that somewhere in the conversation I would have asked him what about the time when he could no longer cheat death? And what has he laid in store on the other side? He admitted that he believed in God. I would have reminded him that one day soon he will have to meet him. What preparation has he made for that?

"Again, Tom is very proud of his business record. He sought to hide behind a few bad business experiences with some Christians. I think that I would have asked him if he ever sold a new Chevy that turned out to be a "lemon." Then I would have reminded him that he was not dishonest and that all Chevys are not bad, although the customer in this incidence was unhappy. Why then should he condemn the church because of a few "lemons"?

"But more than that, I would have reminded him that I didn't come to tell him about church members, even the best ones, but about Christ. And even though some professing Christians may not be all that they should be, no one has ever found anything wrong with Christ, because he was perfect.

"Still further, Tom idolizes his wife. Didn't he say, 'There goes the queen of all the earth'?

"I would have reminded him that it is her Christian faith that makes her what she is. Also his wife is praying that he'll be saved. Perhaps God gave her back to him from her illness so that she might live to see him become a Christian. And if he did so, Christ would make their love for each other sweeter than Tom had ever known.

"Of course, you're well aware that he shut you off rather abruptly. But it has been my experience that this often means that you're getting under the skin and into the heart. Sometimes, evil men are at their worst just before surrendering to Christ. He may be like one of those bass out at Miller's Lake. He's making one last desperate effort to throw off the hook.

"I believe that it would have been well had you prayed with Tom before you left. But apparently you didn't. At any rate you can continue to pray for him. Perhaps it might be well if you let the Holy Spirit do his work with what you did today. Why not just drop by every once in a while and visit with Tom? You might even take him fishing. Or perhaps talk about his flowers. Drink a lot of that strong coffee with him. Win his confidence. Let him know that you are concerned about *him* and not about his 'scalp.'

"And, by the way, if either of you owns a Chevy, why not drive it the next time you go to see Tom. You'll be surprised in the mysterious ways the Lord works his wonders to perform."

G. Avery Lee . . .

Diagnosis.—The writer's descriptive ability causes me to like Tom Hefley, just as he is—a man of orderliness and precision, with a delightful sense of humor that reveals much warmth. His "sharp tongue" reputation does not come through in this episode, unless it is when he is pointing out the ethical failures of Christians he knows. Why are we to assume that Tom isn't happy? Everything describes him as a happy, contented man.

Why this preoccupation with failure on the part of the visitors? Both Bill and Jim were afraid at the beginning. Why? Tom's reputation? Their own uncertainty? A feeling that Tom doesn't need what they are selling? Why the mood of blame at the end for muddying the water?

Was this the first time Bill and Jim had ever talked with Tom? Had they ever done business with him? Has the church pestered the "bejeebers" out of him? Tom sounds like the kind of person who, in former years, the pastor would always take the visiting evangelist around to see. Sensing his own failure, the pastor would hope a stranger could do the job for him.

Why does Tom have the feeling that, even in hospital visitation, the pastor is merely doing a job he is paid to do?

Relationship.—The next time, if there is a next time, don't be so sudden! There is much question about the approach of going without notifying him ahead of time. This is too important a matter for "shot-in-the-dark chance-takings." Until Tom Hefley sees or experiences a need for what these men have, they cannot possibly sell him. They have done nothing even to plant seed in that direction. These men came to plant seed and gather the crop all in one session. Even nature takes several months!

The one chance Bill and Jim had was when Tom started pouring out his bitterness about dealing with crooked church people. And they stopped him. Why not say, "We don't like it either, Tom. We wish it weren't this way. Tell us more of your feelings." Once he got all the poisonous grit out of his craw, he would have *felt* better. Then there could have been a more positive discussion.

With their mood of failure, their emotion of fear, and Jim's anxiety about losing his temper, it is doubtful that Bill and Jim can establish the kind of relationship with Tom that will be meaningful.

Prescription.—If anyone is going to penetrate Tom's armor, it is Jane his wife. There is a touching tenderness about his love for her.

Just going to see Tom Hefley at revival time, or on the regular visitation night, isn't going to get the job done. He already suspects that his scalp is wanted as a trophy and, cagey as he is, having been hunted all these years, the wily old fellow knows all the tricks to evade the hunter.

Tom deserves a hearty, "touché" about his belief in God and Christ, and for turning the argument right back on his visitors. And, you know, he is right about not having to join the church. Pulling the Bible on him isn't going to work, either. He evidently knows what the Bible contains.

Tom Hefley would understand shooting straight from the hip; so, someone whom he does trust and respect will need to level with him, not sneak up on his blind side.

One even suspects that Tom is a Christian who takes great delight in tormenting his tormenters and enjoys the thrill of the chase. But he isn't going to allow others the pleasure of taking his scalp. If I preached his funeral, I'd probably do it with the viewpoint that Tom was a believer in God and Christ, albeit an unidentified one.

EDITOR'S NOTE.—How would you witness to this person?

5

"I'm About at the End of My Rope"

Albert L. Meiburg

Nick Davenport comes from a good family. His parents are among the older and more respected citizens of Belleview, a city of 100,000.

The majority of people instinctively like Nick on their first contact. He is genial, enthusiastic, and outgoing. He likes football, hunting, a good joke, and a beer now and then.

Nick and I have had a great deal in common. Together, we started working for old Mr. Baldwin the same year. We were both just out of college and eager to learn the construction business. You might say that we worked our way from the ground up—literally—because that first summer, we dug hundreds of footings. It was all part of the Baldwin philosophy that to direct others you have to do a little bit of everything that they have to do.

We griped a great deal to one another during those lean, hard years. We simmered under some pretty dull foremen. Old Mr. Baldwin wasn't inclined to take many suggestions from a couple of just-out-of-college engineers. And Dottie and Ann, our wives, had their hands full trying to reconcile our hourly wages with our executive tastes. So, it helped tremendously just to be able to share our common frustrations.

Gradually, our lot improved. Baldwin Construction Company rode the crest of the postwar building boom, and Nick and I rode with it. We became gang bosses, foremen, and finally, supervising engineers.

Funny thing, though, as things got better for us, we seemed to have less in common. For one thing, our work usually took us to scattered parts of the state. We saw each other only on rare occasions in the "big" office.

Our families sort of drifted apart, too. Nick and Dottie traveled with a set of folks whose ways were a little more uninhibited than Ann and I cared for. So, little by little, we saw less of them.

Although Nick and Dottie had been members of our Sunday School class in the old days, I was not sure that Nick had ever made a public profession of faith.

As their income increased, Nick and Dottie became more involved in the Jaycees and the Sertoma Club, and less and less regular in Sunday School.

When they first began to miss, I tried friendly reminders. "We've been missing you at church," I'd say. The next Sunday, they'd be back. But it wouldn't be long before a convention or conclave of some sort would take them away again, and they finally quit coming.

I had heard rumors around the office that Nick's work was slipping, too. The word was too vague to really mean much, and I hate to pry into matters which don't really concern me. Still, I worried when I heard that Nick's monthly reports were a week late, or that he was a month behind schedule on a school job down in Oak Grove, or that he had failed to show up at an important Monday supervisors' meeting.

So, I wasn't really surprised when after a Monday meeting recently, Nick came over and asked if I had any plans for lunch. I needed to get out on a job early that afternoon, but there is always time for lunch so we walked around to a neighborhood restaurant.

After our usual, good-natured cutting, there was a pause. Then Nick said, "I guess you've heard that I'm in bad with 'Old Baldy.' "

"I'm not sure exactly what you mean, Nick," I replied, honestly. "I had heard something about some hang-ups on one of your jobs or something, but I don't put too much faith in the office grapevine."

"Well," he continued. "It's worse than just a late completion date. You know I've always had my problems with the 'old man,' but this morning he leveled with me, and I'm afraid maybe you all are going to need a good construction engineer before long."

"That bad?" I responded, with raised eyebrows.

"Yeah, that bad. Look, Greg, we've been through a lot together, right? You haven't forgotten those pick-and-shovel days, have you, and how we used to reorganize the company every evening? Huh?"

"How could I forget?" I smiled.

"Well," Nick continued. "I know we haven't seen much of each other lately, but, well, things have sort of piled up on me and I thought maybe if we could get together like in the old days, maybe it would help."

"What's bothering the 'old man'?" I asked.

Nick put his fork down and raised both hands above the table before furiously answering: "He started by chewing me out for missing a couple of Monday sessions, like I was a schoolboy and he was the teacher!"

"I can believe it," was my comment. I knew that Mr. Baldwin was a stickler for punctuality.

Nick needed little encouragement as the words and feeling rolled out: "Then he got on the Oak Grove School job. Sure, it's overdue. But he doesn't understand that I can't control the weather! And I'm not going to have the crews doing things in bad weather which only have to be done over later. So, maybe I haven't been on the site every day—is that any reason to make me personally responsible for the weather?"

"You've missed some time?" I asked.

"What have you heard about my absences? That I've been drinking too much?" Nick bristled.

"I was just trying to get straight about your being on the job," I replied, aware that I had unsuspectingly touched a tender spot.

"Well, it's true that I have missed a few days," he conceded. "After all, if a guy has to get out in all kinds of weather he's going to catch a cold now and then, right? I mean a guy has a right to be sick, doesn't he?"

"Have you been sick?" I asked, matter-of-factly.

"Sure," he declared. "Ask Dr. Robinson if I haven't been to see him. As a matter of fact, he's got me taking some nerve pills right now. He knows what a strain I've been under—not only from Baldwin, but, if I can speak frankly—Dottie and I have been having some trouble, too."

Nick noticed that this revelation caught me off guard.

"I know you're surprised," he continued. "We've managed to keep it pretty private, but it's going to come out now, no way to avoid it.

"Dottie left me last week—took the children and went to Atlanta. You don't know what I've been through since then. I just can't understand it. God knows I've tried to provide for that girl. I've taken Baldwin's gaff when I felt like walking right off the job—would have, too, if it hadn't been for her and the kids.

"She wanted a new house. We got a new house. She wanted new furniture. We got new furniture. She wanted to join the Country Club. We joined the Country Club. Now, here I am, with a house full of expensive furniture, and no family, and she's down in Atlanta. . . ."

The tone of Nick's voice and the tears in his bloodshot eyes showed his desperation.

"Perhaps Dottie's just visiting her folks," I offered.

"No, she's not there," he said dejectedly. "I've tried every day to call her, but they claim she's not there and they won't give me any address. I think Mother and Dad know where she is, too, but they just say that this is something we will have to work out, and they won't help me. I've got to get some word to Dottie, to tell her that I've seen my mistakes, and to convince her that if she'll only come back we can get everything straightened out."

"Everything straightened out?" I echoed.

"Yes," Nick plunged ahead. "I guess in a way drinking *is* involved. You know Dottie has always hated booze. My parents never touched it either. But the way I see it, what's wrong with having a few beers with the boys if it helps everybody relax and have a little fun, see?

"Since Dottie refused to have anything in the house to drink, I started stopping on the way home from work and getting a beer. Just *one* and that's the gospel truth.

"Well, she fussed at me for coming home, smelling of beer. She wouldn't let me kiss her if she could smell it. Sometimes, I'd stop off with the boys, and after I'd had one, I'd think: I'm gonna catch hell for one drink. I might as well have two and get braced. I'll admit that at times I overdid it and came home stinko!

"I knew how Dottie felt before we were married. That's the crazy side of this whole thing. I loved her because she was different, and now I've gone and ruined the whole thing. What can I do? Greg, I'm about at the end of my rope!"

Nick's desperation was beginning to get through to me. He was certainly on the spot, all right. But what could I, a friend, do? I'm not a psychiatrist or preacher, either. And if I didn't get to that new job, the next man up before "Old Baldy" would be me. While I mulled over the predicament, Nick pinned me to the wall.

"Greg, please help me!" he pleaded. "Get Ann to talk to my folks. They think very highly of her. If she could persuade them to give me Dottie's telephone number, I could at least talk with her. You don't know how terrible it is to want to get through to someone and not be able to do so!"

HOW TO WIN THIS PERSON TO CHRIST
Kenneth L. Chafin . . .

Principle.—God knows what each person is like and in spite of that loves him and wants him to be his child.

More and more, those of us who are in the church are going to be confronted by individuals who are in exactly the same position as Nick—potential family breakup, potential loss of job, breakdown of personality, and alcoholism.

First, the values and goals of the "young executives" ran crosswise to the values and goals of the family in which Nick was reared. This set him up for a conflict and a sense of inadequacy and made him a natural for alcoholism.

Second, there was no one big moment of renouncing the church and the values of the church, but a gradual drift in a different position and with a different pattern. Nick has found himself one more victim of a "success pattern" which is basically destructive.

Third, we face a big danger in oversimplifying the source of Nick's problem. His parents may have done just this. We do not know. It is more than drinking. It is what is behind the drink. The alcoholism cannot be ignored, but it must not blind us to the larger problem.

Also, there is much we need to know. We are told nothing about what spiritual resources there are in Nick's experience. If he followed the pattern, he probably joined the church before entering high school. While Nick may have drifted from his teachings, they are there. While he may have viewed them rather negatively, his early teachings do represent a source of help. His desire to recall the early days of the friendship might suggest a desire to remember early days in the church.

How can another individual communicate to Nick the fact that God knows all about him and all of his troubles but still loves him and has a plan for his life? What will convince Nick that there can be forgiveness and acceptance and new life and a beginning again with God?

First, he desperately needs a friend who does not make conditions on his friendship. His boss makes conditions. His wife make conditions. His parents make conditions. Because he so desperately needs the approval of all of them, and doesn't feel that he has measured up, Nick is trying to hide in the bottle.

Second, Nick needs help in seeing that God still accepts him. If one friend who knows all about him still accepts him, and that friend urges him to turn his life to God, then Nick is likely to believe. Get him to pray honestly to God and to talk with God about all of his problems.

Third, get Nick to deal realistically with the problem of drink. While other things are behind it, drink is now creating its own problems. Whether Nick needs help from Alcoholics Anonymous or from some professional counseling would have to be determined. But he desperately needs to realize that he cannot face life through the bottle.

Finally, if his parents are available, try to interpret to them where Nick is in his pilgrimage, and enlist their help. Get in contact with his wife and let her know that he is seeking help.

The seeking of a spiritual relationship with God can be

the experience that helps Nick to deal with problems related to his wife, job, family, and drink. This has been true with countless other people.

Herschel H. Hobbs . . .

Nick Davenport cannot stand success. That is his basic problem. Where adversity has slain its thousands, prosperity has slain its tens of thousands. And Nick is about to add to that latter number. He is not antagonistic toward religion. But his prosperity has led him away from old friends and practices to venture into a new world. His wife went with him, but neither of them anticipated the dire result. Even though his wife strongly objected to strong drink, Nick indulged anyway. His outgoing nature made him susceptible to alcoholism. First, a few beers, then more, then occasional drunkenness. Finally, a crisis was created in his job and family. When "the roof fell in" on him, Nick turned to his old church friend for help. He reluctantly admitted that "in a way drinking *is* involved." In self-pride, he put it that way. But it is evident that he recognized it as his real problem. This is seen in his admission that he is at the end of his rope. He wants help. And because of his desire for help, the battle is half won. But how to give help to him?

In dealing with Nick, I would not berate him about what drinking has done to him. He is well aware of that. So, I would concentrate on two things which are evident in his case.

First, Nick is a builder. I would talk to him in a language that he understands. He knows the importance of a good foundation for a building and of using good materials in its construction. I would point out to him his knowledge of these facts. Then I would remind him kindly that he had used faulty materials in building the house of his life simply because he had not erected it upon the proper foundation.

Having done so, I would ask Nick to read with me the words of Jesus found in Matthew 7:24–27. This, of course, is the story of the wise and foolish men who built their houses on rock and sand, respectively. The former heard Jesus' sayings and did them; the latter heard but did not do or respond. I would observe that Jesus, too, was a builder and knew the importance of the foundation.

I would point out to Nick that both houses underwent the same storms; one stood but the other fell. I would remind him that prosperity can be a greater storm in an individual's life than adversity. Then, on the basis of our friendship, I would recall the old days and how we started out together, and had risen together in the economic scale. Without apology, I would cite the present differences in our situations. My job is secure and my home is happy. He is about to lose his job and his home is broken. Both of us have experienced the storm of *prosperity.* But with far different results. Why? Because of the different foundations upon which we have built. I have built my life upon Christ the Rock; Nick has built his upon other things or sand.

I would turn to 1 Corinthians 3:11, and read aloud, "For other foundation can no man lay than that is laid, which is Jesus Christ." In this respect, I would tell Nick that in order to set his life in order he needs to start with a new foundation as he receives Jesus Christ as his Saviour. I would explain Jesus' atoning death and resurrection to Nick, endeavoring to get him to trust in Christ for salvation.

Second, Nick has said, "You don't know how terrible it is to want to get through to somebody and not be able to!" I would remind him that his present greatest need is to "get through" to the Lord, and he knows his number. "Believe on the Lord Jesus Christ, and thou shalt be saved, and thy house" (Acts 16:31).

I would point out that what Dottie wants is a changed husband. And only Jesus can do that. Once that change has taken place we could get word to Dottie—yes, and to "Old Baldy." That word would doubtless change the situation with both his home and job.

Of course, I would have to press for a decision. I would appeal to Nick's love for his family, but most of all I would help him understand the Lord's love for him. In my experience, I have found that if you can get someone to pray for salvation, he will usually open his heart to the Lord. In Nick's present condition, I believe that he would make such a decision.

G. Avery Lee . . .

Diagnosis.—Nick Davenport is in a real crisis. He has lost his family and is about to lose his job. He is face-to-face with failure—failure as a man and as a professional. Although Nick is pouring out his soul, is he just feeling sorry for himself, or is he genuinely concerned about straightening up? We get the feeling that Nick is not only diagnosing his own case, but also prescribing his own treatment. Nick is not yet in grief because he has not accepted his loss. Component parts of the alcoholic are fantasy and unreality. How can firmness and tenderness be used to bump him with reality?

Despite his wife's abhorrence of drinking, she drifted along with Nick. Perhaps she was trying to keep him stable. It is more likely, however, that she got vicarious enjoyment from the faster life. She liked and wanted the Country Club life. Her nagging and prudish, self-righteous "lips that touch liquor shall never touch mine" rules alienated him and sent him off to others.

Relationship.—Alcoholics are such lovable scoundrels because they are tender. Nick has been my friend for years. He needs me now. I must not betray his confidence and let him down. Neither can I be caught and manipulated into being his friend on such dictated terms as, "Get Ann to talk to Dottie." Nor can I change my role of friend so that Nick attaches himself to me as a "Big Daddy."

Whether or not I am a social drinker has not been brought out. If I am a teetotaller, do I look down my blue nose at Nick's red one? Much depends upon how I react to Nick. Patience is called for, because Nick will probably slip off the wagon if he gets on. It is hard for the controlled social drinker or for the total abstainer to be patient with the alcoholic.

The pastor needs to be brought in, for this is a task

which I cannot do alone. With Nick's willingness, a pastoral conference can be arranged.

I can be an emissary to Dottie, not to bring her back, but to take the message that Nick is seeking help and to ask if she will help. And I must be unshakable at this point!

Prescription.—Nick knows what he has to do—*quit drinking!* This may be the time for the direct frontal approach instead of the nondirective, permissive technique. Now may be the time to confront Nick directly with his need of Christ. Whatever his reasons for not having made a profession of faith should be brought out in the open and faced. This is the role of the pastor. Accepting Christ as Saviour may not immediately solve Nick's drinking problem or get his wife back, but that is the place of beginning. Even "Old Baldy" would go along with this and give Nick another chance—*one!*

Someway, Dottie must get back in the picture. She needs to see her contribution to the problem and face up to it. Her pushing the Country Club life and her nagging have compounded the problem. Dottie needs help to understand her place. *Alanon* (wives of alcoholics) would help her. But, of course, Dottie cannot be brought back on manipulative terms.

Nick may not need Alcoholics Anonymous yet, but he does need a new set of acquaintances. There is a ready-made group at the old church, if he can face them, and if they will accept and love him.

EDITOR'S NOTE.—How would you witness to Nick Davenport?

6

"Christianity Is the White Man's Religion"

W. T. Moore

Wayne Scott dressed for work thoughtfully. He had been on night duty just two nights. He and Thomas Williams, his new squad car partner, had been fairly busy those two nights but today a bitter cold wave had descended on the city and he knew that they would probably have more time to talk tonight. It was of his partner that he thought as he got ready for work.

As a policeman in a city of a quarter million people that had had its share of racial problems, Wayne had become interested in human relations. However, it was really something his pastor had said that helped lead him to volunteer for assignment with a Negro policeman. The pastor had said: "We know Negroes as servants, or think about them as problems. As equals they are usually strangers to us." Also, there had been a statement in a recent meeting of the men's group in his church, "Mission Action is to help us reach people who are unlike us."

Wayne had learned that Thomas was not a Christian but did not know why. He had been pleased by Thomas' friendly spirit, especially the way Thomas had put him at ease about using first names, because Wayne had studied in the police human relations course about how Negroes resented this. He had also learned that Thomas was a college graduate and was ambitious. "I hope to be police chief of this city someday," he had said, and the way he explained it Wayne felt it was a reasonable ambition. "You see, this city will have a Negro majority in another ten years. We will continue to have racial troubles. I'll have to take some hard knocks for a while from Negroes who look on a Negro policeman as a tool of the whites, but eventually there will be a large number of Negroes on the police force. Because of overcrowding, economics, poorer schools, and other reasons, the crime rate is higher in the Negro community. Someday, the whites will want to see if a Negro can do anything about the crime. A Negro policeman who keeps a clean record and prepares himself ought to be chief someday." A sound of bitterness came into his voice then when he added, "Of course, an awful lot of 'ought to be's' fail to happen to Negroes."

Later, as they cruised deserted streets, Wayne talked about his church and the mission project he had helped in on his days off. Thomas listened silently and finally Wayne ventured:

"Did you go to church when you were growing up?"

"Yeah, my grandmother took me to church all the time—I kind of liked it, though. I thought there was something to it then."

"You don't think there's anything to it now?"

Thomas, who was driving, paused to listen to the police radio, then as they stopped at a red light, studied Wayne's face as if to determine if his answer would shock him.

"No, I don't. I first began to have some doubts when I realized that some preachers were exploiting the people to line their own pockets. Then I realized how separate Negro and white churches were and began to ask myself if there was a white God and a black God. You may say that there are separate churches because we worship differently, but that's only a crutch. Negroes did leave the white churches to form their own, but they did it because they were only associate members and never had full membership rights.

"When I was in college, there was an African student there who was refused by a church of the denomination that had sent out the missionaries that had won him to Christ. The fact that churches are changing only after sports, entertainment, the armed services, public accommodations and schools have changed proves what I am saying."

Thomas had warmed to his subject and now he paused as if to indicate that he hadn't meant anything personal.

It was time for their middle of the shift break and they swung into an all-night restaurant. It was deserted so Wayne decided to further the conversation.

"Then segregation and hypocrisy of white churches is the main factor that caused you to turn against Christianity?" Wayne asked.

"Well, it wasn't until I got in college and began to study history the way it really happened that I fully realized that Christianity is the white man's religion. Oh, I know there have been individuals who were exceptions, just as I have known some whites who treated me right; but collectively the white race has always taken advantage of the

Negro. It was the white Christian nations that carried on the slave trade. White preachers tried to justify slavery from the Bible—just as some of them try to justify segregation from the Bible today. Have you ever read Negro newspapers?"

Surprised at the question, Wayne replied, "I've seen them but I can't say that I ever really read them."

"You ought to read the society section of a Negro newspaper and find out how many light-skinned Negroes there are, because there are a great many more than most whites realize. This didn't come from intermarriage and most of it didn't happen recently. Most of it came from slavery and from those years when the white man could impose his will on Negro women.

"I knew a white man who admitted to me that his father, a deacon, had participated in a lynching. This man was ashamed of it but what kind of religion did his father have?"

Thomas did not pause for an answer. "Most Negroes believe that any white man who comes into the Negro community comes for no good purpose.

"The colonial powers that ruled so much of the world were the white powers. In India, China, Africa, and even America, the missionary went first to lull people to sleep—then the white powers took slaves, land, or wealth from these lands. A 'Christian' power profited from the narcotics trade in China and even fought a war to continue the opium trade.

"The black man in America has in many ways been a better Christian than the white man and what has it gotten him? In the white man's hands, in the white man's interpretation—where has Christianity brought this world? It has brought the nonwhite (two thirds of the human population) to rebellion. Two thirds of the human population today is telling the one third minority white man, 'Get out!' And the white man is leaving. As he leaves, we see the nonwhite people returning in a rush to their original religions, which had been labeled 'pagan' by the conquering white man."

Again, Thomas had become carried away with his subject. Now he looked at his partner hesitantly and said: "Wayne, I like you and I think we can make a good team. I know you believe in Christianity and I don't. Maybe we ought not to talk about religion."

Wayne thought quickly to himself: If I ever am to influence this man I must keep this an open subject. Breathing a prayer he said: "I agree with part of what you are saying. Some of it I don't know enough history to be sure about, but I am interested in why you feel the way you do. You won't offend me." He paused and then observed: "Your feelings seem to be similar to those of the Black Muslims."

Thomas paused before answering. "I think they have found a truth in their rejection of Christianity. But their religion is foreign to America—and I'm an American! Sure, I'm proud to know that there were advanced civilizations in Africa when Europeans were still living in caves, but that doesn't mean I'm going to dress or live like an African. My forefathers came to America earlier than many of the white's forefathers. Mine came against their will, but we helped build this land, and I for one am a true part of America. I intend to stay that way."

Wayne thought to himself, I wonder if he would be a Muslim if it did not stand in the way of his ambitions.

Thomas continued: "As I see it, the white man's Christianity has been used to brainwash the Negro. We've been led to fix our eyes on pie in the sky while whites enjoyed their heaven here. Christianity among the Negroes has been an escape, and also an Uncle Tom device to help him please the white man. Of course, the majority of Negroes have been sincere in accepting Christianity, but they were also blind to what white Christianity was doing with them in the world. Christianity is the only religion in the world that has segregated people by color."

Wayne observed: "I've heard it said that Christ wasn't white the way we think of whites today; and didn't the Christians of New Testament times include people of many races?"

"Perhaps so. I read that when Billy Graham was questioned in Africa he said: 'I believe in Christ, not Christianity'; but I'm not so sure you can separate the two. Maybe Christianity did include all men on an equal basis one time, but it sure has changed. Whites have made Christianity the white man's religion. Those who have accepted it in Asia and Africa often did so because it pleased those in power.

"You know the Black Muslims believe the white man is the devil race. I've seen enough deviltry among my people that I don't believe whites have a corner on hellishness. I just think Christianity got corrupted so much by racism that it is hopeless."

HOW TO WIN THIS PERSON TO CHRIST
Kenneth L. Chafin . . .

Principle.—To witness means to expose ourselves to others. This means that we not only talk but listen.

Sometimes, our willingness to listen without getting mad or striking back will do more to communicate the gospel than what we say. If God loved us enough to be born into this world and to expose himself to us even while we were sinners, then we need to love people enough to be willing to sit with them and expose ourselves to them even though they, too, are sinners.

I have a hard time seeing Thomas as a whole person. He seems to be more of a composite of a number of young Negroes whom I have met.

It would be an understatement to say that Thomas is a very troubled and confused young man. He overlooks a host of white Christians who have championed his cause at great cost to themselves. He also fails to appreciate a host of splendid Negro Christians. Half of the Negroes in America are Baptists. These Negro churches have had some great pastors who have led their people to take giant strides during the past decades.

There are several general suggestions I would make about dealing with Thomas and persons like Thomas. *First,* I do not think we ought to try to defend the white church and the white community. Much that we have done is not defensible. Then too, his problems are much more emotional than rational.

Second, I think we should not strike back about racism

in reverse. The Negro community is also a fragmented community with many voices calling for people to follow. Thomas is typical of many Negro young people who have taken the hurt of their race into themselves.

Because God loves us as we are, with no strings attached, I would suggest that Wayne make every effort to accept Thomas with all of his bitterness. Thomas probably does not even believe all that he has said. The words are sometimes like records, a collection of all the accusations that have ever been made against the church.

I think it would be good somewhere in the discussion to point out that Christianity is a world religion with one Creator and one Saviour and one church. It would also be good to point out that God is a God of love and acceptance who forgives people and gives meaning to life. The love of God is not invalidated by the lovelessness of an individual Christian or congregation.

I think it would be helpful to find out a little more about Thomas' background. How did a boy, reared by a grandmother, go to college? Who helped? Who cared? Who prayed? Who shared? In all likelihood, he has a very warm spot for some people who had faith in him and faith in God and were responsible for this opportunity.

I think it would be very wise to find a sharp Negro pastor who could help in giving a witness to Thomas. Right now I do not think the white church has a chance with large-scale evangelism with Negroes. But where we can, we should join with Negro churches and Negro church members in a cooperative witness. At least, the Negro pastor would not have the racial factor to overcome.

I would continue to pray for Thomas and build that kind of relationship which would allow him to be exactly the way that he is and still be loved. He needs to be in touch with this kind of love.

Herschel H. Hobbs . . .

Obviously, this is the most difficult case analyzed thus far. The difficulty lies in the fact that so much that Thomas says is true. He shows the evidence of his college training, and he has learned well his lesson in past and current history. It is evident that one conversation about religion or Christianity will not be able to break through all of the barriers that are in his mind and heart. So, patience and understanding are necessary if he is to be reached for Christ. However, certain factors evolved in this first conversation which serve as beginning points.

In dealing with Thomas, I would not debate the issues. I would agree with him that history reveals a sordid story as to how white men and nations have wronged Negroes and other groups. I would also acknowledge with regret that the churches have not been in the lead in solving racial problems. But these things have not always been one-way streets. I would take the position that there were/are perversions of the Christian gospel. I would remind him that as a child he had liked what he learned in church. And that is basic in Christian truth.

At this point I would remind Thomas that I was not talking to him about *Christianity,* but about *Christ.* I would press the point that Christ was neither white nor black, but probably brown—which incidentally is a median point in color between white and black. I would remind him that Jesus came to save all men, not just some men. With this I would read John 3:16: "God so loved the world . . ." Then John 4:42, "This is indeed the Christ, the Saviour of the world."

I would ask Thomas why the world or men need a Saviour. (Because of sin.) I would point out that the difference between us is not the color of our skins. It is that I am a sinner saved by grace and he is a sinner who is lost outside the grace of God. I would explain sin and what Christ did to save us from it; and that Thomas must trust in Jesus to be saved.

Thomas is ambitious in a worthy manner. On this basis I would tell him that the basic teaching of the Bible about man is that he is the object of God's love, and is of infinite worth and dignity before God. From Matthew 16:26, I would show him that to reject Christ in gaining the whole world to the loss of his soul would be the worst of bargains. However, if he receives Christ, he becomes a child of God, an heir of God, and a joint-heir with Christ (Rom. 8:17). I would then read to him Galatians 3:28: "There is neither Jew nor Greek, there is neither bond nor free, there is neither male nor female: for ye are all one in Christ Jesus." I would explain that this is the Christian ideal and that anything short of this is contrary to the will of God.

Thomas made reference to missionaries. I think that I would endeavor to show him that in the period of colonial expansion the missionaries traveled with explorers and exploiters simply because there was no other way available by which to carry the gospel to lost men in those areas of the earth. But I would cite also modern missionaries, men such as David Livingstone and Bill Wallace who literally gave their lives for people of other races. Furthermore, I would point out that it was the Christian gospel of man's worth and dignity before God which was the root of the unrest in Africa and elsewhere. The trouble is not the gospel, but not enough of it. I would also point out the tribute paid to missionaries by the Nigerian government for the part played by them in bringing about an orderly transition from colonialism to freedom. I would cite the many Negroes who are leaders in various Christian bodies over the world, including Dr. William R. Tolbert, Jr., a Liberian, who is the President of the Baptist World Alliance. He was elected by acclamation to this post by world Baptists, not meeting in Africa but in Miami Beach, Florida, the Deep South of the United States. I would point out that only the Spirit of Christ could form such a fellowship among men of different races and cultures.

But, in the final analysis, the Christian experience is a personal one. So, I would seek to show Thomas that, despite social injustices, he needs Christ as a person.

Furthermore, Thomas said that he liked Wayne as a person. If I were Wayne I would tell him what Christ and my church had done for me so that I could relate to him as a *man,* not as a Negro.

One example is worth many sermons. Therefore, I would so relate to Thomas that through the warmth of my Christian love his antagonisms would gradually disappear. If we can live together as *men* through my Christian faith, how much more so if we both love and serve Christ? And if we, why not others?

I would constantly pray for Thomas and use every opportunity to witness *naturally,* but most of all to *be* a witness to him. The smog of his unfortunate experiences could not forever resist that.

G. Avery Lee . . .

Diagnosis.—Thomas Williams has just cause for believing that Christianity is a white man's religion. Too much evidence is in his favor. While many white Christians do not believe this, too many others demonstrate it. Even in our overseas missions, we transplant too much of our own cultural patterns, including architecture and organizational structure, as well as social customs.

Tom says that he is rejecting *all* Christianity—both white and Negro churches. His reasons sound legitimate. However, could these be cover-ups because he just doesn't want to go to church; doesn't want anything to do with religious faith of any kind? He is rejecting the Black Muslim religion, too. We say that some white men use the cover of "hypocrites in the church," or "I was forced to go as a child" to rationalize their lack of Christian acceptance. Why not Tom's form of 'racism'?

Tom borders on a paranoia focused on whites. He is bent on correcting wrongs with a vengeance. *But,* Christianity still lets him know that he cannot have the luxury of hate. He doesn't think that he can be accepted by a 'white god'; what about a 'black god'? Take all whites off the scene and his anger will take a new focus, toward lighter or darker Negroes, perhaps.

This thoughtful, ambitious young man is an educated, sophisticated racist in reverse. And, from his point of view, this is not an irrational approach. From our point of view, we would say that his prejudiced knowledge of history and sociology has been selected to fit his way of thinking. Our problem is to get him to see something else.

Relationship.—Let us give Wayne a great deal of credit for a good beginning. He at least got the conversation going and showed a willingness to listen to an outpouring of bitterness long bottled up. Can he drain off some more? Why not admit that both men are prejudiced? Wayne will have a great deal of ingrained prejudice of his own to overcome. If he can get his feelings openly verbalized, as Tom has done, and if Tom is as willing to listen, we might have a chance.

As police officers, these two men will see the seamier side of human behavior, both Negro and white. How Wayne reacts in the squad car toward the Negro law violators, as well as to the white ones, will reveal the inner man. Whether he acts with firm compassion or with coarse brutality will intensify Tom's feelings. There is no place for a double standard of treatment on Wayne's part, not if he wants to have a Christian influence on Tom.

Much will depend upon the attitude of Wayne's wife, as well as that of his pastor. What if Wayne does gain a hearing from Tom, will he be able to invite him to his church? If he does, and Tom is rejected, what then?

This situation calls for patience and an overdose of

kindness. Every virtue mentioned in 2 Peter 1:5–8 is called for. These virtues just might keep those who work with Tom from "being ineffective or unfruitful in the knowledge of our Lord Jesus Christ."

Prescription.—Let's face it: The chances of getting Tom into the Christian faith are an "impossible possibility." Humanly speaking, there is little to go on. But the grace of God can, and does, work in human lives. It is doubtful if any white man, or white church, can reach Tom, and he has rejected the Negro church. However, a respected Negro Christian could be brought in on this case. Tom's fond early memories of church are in our favor, but mountainous obstacles are in the way. In all likelihood, the white church and white Christians have the better opportunity.

Tom believes that Christianity is tied to a specific culture; and he, too, is right. Now, can he be shown otherwise? As an educated man, he might follow a planned reading course—if a right program can be outlined. In this large city there is probably a college. Some Christians from other nations, especially African or Asian, could be invited to dinner at Wayne's house. Tom would also be invited. These Christians could help him dispel the cultural bias. Then he could learn what is essential to Christian faith and what is superficial.

Unless Wayne's wife, his pastor, and his church show a true Christian attitude, we are in for failure.

EDITOR'S NOTE.—How would you witness to Thomas?

7

"Chaplain, What Really Bugs Me Is Being Alone"

Clifford Ingle

Sgt. Fred Herndon was in his mid-twenties, a career soldier, expertly trained and experienced in military tactics. He was one of the assigned personnel in an Army Camp which was a Training Center for army inductees (those from civilian life into military service). For some sixteen weeks he had helped in giving the inductees basic training which was to prepare them for assignments to regular units which were serving in various parts of the United States and the world.

Sgt. Herndon's ability in leadership was obvious and outstanding. In my normal checking of records as Chaplain, I noticed that Sgt. Herndon had written "none" in the space following "religious preference."

One morning when I was making the normal rounds, I met Sgt. Herndon at the small arms firing range. The men of his company were waiting their turn to fire. He was sitting on the ground somewhat apart from his men.

He arose as I approached and I introduced myself and suggested that we both sit down. He became engaged in general conversation involving such things as hometown, length and places of military service, and the war. Then I turned the conversation by saying, "Sgt. Herndon, as I have observed you in training the new inductees I have been so impressed by your leadership that I wanted to know more about you. All inquires have verified that you are an excellent soldier. However, one thing has left me disturbed."

"What's that, Chaplain?"

"It is," I replied, "that seemingly you have no religious affiliation, or to be more specific you have not become a Christian. Is this so?"

"That's right Chaplain," he continued. "Look, you and I both know that the basic principle of warfare is victory over an enemy. To put it bluntly it means killing. Now I know your job is not to carry a gun, but the rest of us do and for one purpose—to kill."

"Yes," I replied, "I know that war is a cruel, brutal, killing business and that any sane and sensible person abhors it."

"See those men over there flat on their bellies," he interrupted. "Those men are shooting at targets for one simple reason. Those targets represent the enemy. In a few days or weeks they will probably be shooting at the real thing. Now Chaplain, it's my job to see that they know how to shoot straight." He paused for a moment then continued, "Tell me honestly Chaplain, do you see any place in war for religion or this Christ who is supposed to save everybody?"

I replied to the effect that Christ's presence and salvation was not determined by or dependent on situations or circumstances and that he (Christ) could be and was just as much in the lives of his followers who were on their bellies on the firing line as when they might be in the chapel or in civilian life.

Fred evidently missed the point as he said, "Come on Chaplain, don't give me that stuff. You mean that Christ is out there leaning over each Christian soldier and whispering in his ear, 'Atta boy, you got him right through the heart. Now get the next one between the eyes.' Oh boy, that's a good one."

"Did you hear me say such a thing?" I asked. "To be a Christian does not mean that Jesus approves of everything we do or may be required to do. In fact. . . ."

He interrupted and said, "Chaplain, I guess it's all right for a soldier to be a Christian. That's his business just as long as it doesn't interfere with his being a good soldier. But me! I can't buy it.

"Look, I've been in war. I've been wounded two times. I've killed the enemy. War makes you act like an animal. Pretty soon you feel that you are shooting animals. Man, don't talk to me about religion at a time like that." He paused and then continued, "I remember when I read about some soldier saying that there were no atheists in foxholes, I just laughed out loud."

"Let me ask you Sergeant, who do you think Jesus Christ really is? Tell me just exactly what kind of a person you think him to be," I said.

"Hmm," he paused, shrugged his shoulders and said, "You know this stumps me. Honestly, I have never thought about this. I don't ever remember being asked such a question."

He paused for almost a minute. I said nothing.

He continued, "Chaplain, do you want to know what really bothers me? What really bugs me is that I don't like to be alone. Then all my past war experiences keep coming to my mind. I'm OK as long as I'm busy, or down at the PX, or at a movie. (*pause*) Chaplain, take it from me, war is hell. It doesn't make sense. It's stupid and insane, . . . oh there's the signal for me to move my men to the firing range."

We got up from where we had been sitting and he said, "Say, we had quite a talk. I'm glad you came out. This is the first time I've really unloaded. I guess it's good to get it off your chest."

I expressed appreciation for him and our visit and then said, "Sgt. Herndon, may I ask you to do two things? First, really think about who Jesus is. Second, come to the chapel services and just see for yourself what Christianity is. I assure you we won't do anything to embarrass you. I hope to see you Sunday morning at the chapel."

HOW TO WIN THIS PERSON TO CHRIST
Kenneth L. Chafin . . .

Principle.—Find out as much as possible about the spiritual background of a person to whom we witness.

The person understands what we say in the terms of his own background both positively and negatively. Find out where the person was reared. Ask about his family, about early experiences in the church. He usually will not mind sharing this. It will actually help him to verbalize where he has been and the influences that have shaped his present understanding.

There is really not much that we know about the sergeant. The discussion seemed to get too deep, too theological, too philosophical, and too personal, *too soon.* Back up and get acquainted. On the surface, this may seem like a waste of time since it is in the nowness of time that men are converted. But the religious background makes a difference in how a person understands the very terms that we use. In asking questions, there are some principles to keep in mind. *First,* assume the best. This creates a better climate for discussion. *Second,* begin with questions that can be answered with the mind and move toward questions that require the emotion or the will. *Third,* assume the responsibility for communicating. Do not get mad at a person who does not understand what you are asking. Back up and rephrase it in terminology that he is able to understand. Witnessing is not only talking, it is also listening. Sometimes, it is better to control a conversation by asking a good question and listening.

Although I might be wrong, I think the "war is hell" type of discussion is probably a smoke screen for the sergeant. If he were a college student I would be more inclined to feel that this represents a real problem. However, since he is actually training soldiers to perform in war I would suspect that this is something that he has brought up to sidetrack the chaplain.

Human beings often hide their real feelings behind things which do not really bother them very much. If the sergeant can get the person who is witnessing to him to be on the defensive by making some statement like this, then he gets them away from him personally.

My own impression from the small amount of description that we have is that the chaplain should be careful though not to take too lightly the horror of men being trained to kill other human beings. This is especially true today when there seems to be a new questioning of the morality of war inside the church and outside the church.

I think the real clue in the sergeant's conversation is his discussion about hating to be alone. The fact that he has to keep himself busy doing things rather than relating to persons would indicate that he desperately needs not only a relationship with God but also relationships with people that bring joy to his life. This might be a place to make a very valid witness.

While war can never be justified as being the perfect will of God, he is willing to work with man in this imperfect context and to help him. While war is a very terrible thing, it is a context in which some men may find what it means to be alive. We take life so for granted in normal times that sometimes when people are uprooted and have the whole pattern of their lives changed it gives them occasion to really think what life is all about. While in college, I pastored a church which was adjacent to an air force base. Many of the individuals who were in the service and who were going overseas had found in their relationship with God meaning for their lives. I would try to communicate this to the sergeant.

Herschel H. Hobbs . . .

Sgt. Fred Herndon is quite a guy. To say the least, he is forthright and honest. He regards soldiering as killing, yet he has made it his career. And he takes his job seriously. He readily admits that he is not a religious man. In fact, he admits that he has not given it much thought. Except to conclude that a man cannot be a Christian and a "good soldier." It is clear that while he is honest in his thinking, he is confused in many ways. In my judgment, before Sgt. Herndon can be won to Christ, certain things must be cleared up for him.

To begin with, I would seek to show him that there is a difference between killing maliciously and killing in defense of self and country. I would point out to him that the Sixth Commandment has reference to murder. In defensive warfare, normally a soldier does not kill because he enjoys it. He kills in self-defense and to defend his nation and its principles. There are some things worth dying for.

I would ask Fred if he thought it was inconsistent for a

policeman to be a Christian. Anticipating a negative answer, I would point out that a soldier is only a policeman on an international scale whose responsibility it is to resist the evil designs of wicked men. In Fred's training of his men, he was merely enabling them to do their job successfully and with a minimum of personal danger. So, in reality he was saving lives—the lives of his trainees.

Furthermore, can a man be a good soldier and a good Christian at the same time? In reply I would call attention to two *good* soldiers who were great Christians—Robert E. Lee and Stonewall Jackson. I would cite instances of military men in the New Testament who became Christians—Cornelius and numbers of the Praetorian Guard. Thus, I would encourage him to be "a good soldier of Jesus Christ" (2 Tim. 2:3).

Fred showed a lack of understanding as to the meaning of Christ being with an individual regardless of his situation. Therefore, I would seek to show him that there are ways other than encouraging a soldier to kill. There is comfort, courage, and strength of character. The abnormal life of a soldier makes it all the more necessary that he should have the inner fortitude which Christ alone can give.

Fred admitted that he never liked to be alone. On this basis I would mention Jesus' many promises to be with his people. So that in Christ he needs never to be alone. Even his memories of war could be placed at the feet of Jesus, and through confession, Fred could receive forgiveness for his sins.

Touching upon his own wounds I would ask, "Suppose instead that you had been killed. Where would you be now?" From this I would seek to show Fred that he is more than an animal. He is a person who is responsible to God. And eternity for him will be in accord with what he has done with Jesus.

The final statement which Fred made is significant. "I've really unloaded. I guess it's good to get it off your chest." I would say, "Yes, but it is even better to get it off your heart." Then I would explain to him how that could be done—the plan of salvation.

Finally, I would appeal to Fred's interest in his men. He was training them to kill. But some of them would be killed. He was getting them ready to kill. But as a Christian soldier, he could also help to get them ready to die. I would show him what a great responsibility he had both to his country and to his God.

Frankly, I would not expect Fred to grasp all of these things in one session. But I would sow the seed, and then in patient concern I would wait and pray for the harvest. This is not to say that he could and would not receive Christ at once. But I would not be discouraged if he did not.

I would persevere with the firm faith that eventually he would face up to his spiritual need even as he had faced up to the evident conflict between Christ and war.

G. Avery Lee . . .

Diagnosis.—Sherman was right—"War is hell!"—and Sgt. Fred Herndon knows it firsthand. He has been there!

But, is this his only reason for not being a Christian? I suspect that it is not. At any rate, let us respect him for his reason and deal with it until we know more.

Fred Herndon is a sensitive man. This is revealed in his statement, "War makes you feel like an animal. Pretty soon you feel that you are shooting animals." He evidently has a high regard and respect for the value of human life. This is a strong Christian teaching; so make the most of it. Another evidence of his sensitivity is, "I don't like to be alone." Why? No doubt there are some guilt feelings for having shot and killed human beings; so get the guilt feelings out in the open.

The chaplain's question, "Who do you think Jesus Christ really is?" was to the point and stripped away Fred's extraneous arguments. After all, this is the basic question. And every Fred, every chaplain, every analysis writer, every reader must face it and answer it for himself.

However, the chaplain lost his perspective when he gave out a 'program' of action. This is the thing Fred is most likely to reject. In the rejection, he may feel that he is rejecting the chaplain as well as the faith, and in turn will be rejected by God.

Relationship.—The chaplain has a natural entrée. But he also has a difficult role as an officer. He must gain and keep Fred's respect, not only as an officer, but as a man representing God. If the chaplain caters to the officers and centers his activities at the Officers' Club, he will miss out on a vital relationship with the enlisted men. This chaplain seems genuinely interested in all the men of his charge. The fact that he picked Fred out and made a personal effort to see him and find out why he had left the religious preference blank unfilled speaks well for him. True, Fred's record showed unusual qualities, but there is the feeling that the chaplain would do the same for other men.

Fred needs a chance to ponder Jesus Christ, to give him something to think about while he is alone. The chaplain missed a chance to get his foot "in the door" by not saying something like, "Sergeant, do you have any idea why you dread being alone? Think about this and drop around the NCO Club about five o'clock and let's have a sandwich together and talk."

No doubt the chaplain will see Fred again and the continued being together will give friendship a chance to develop. Since this is a stateside camp, there will be opportunities to see Fred in the home setting. If Fred has a wife, the two of them could be invited to the chaplain's residence for dinner. There will be some Christian military men in this camp who could also be invited and give Fred a chance to "talk it out" with his peers.

Prescription.—All men need Christ and the church, just as the opposite is true. Certainly, men of Fred's leadership qualities are needed. We hope he will go to the base chapel. He may not *see* what Christianity is, but the exposure will enable him to *hear* what it is.

The chaplain is the key person. Fred's response to him was good. Having "unloaded," perhaps he can get some more "off his chest." Later on, someone other than the chaplain may reap the harvest.

A dozen years ago a retired lieutenant commander entered college as a freshman. Because his name was the same as mine, I made a visit. It was learned that the man had never made a profession of faith in Christ. However, during his military career he had been active in his attendance and support of chaplains and chapels where he was stationed. He wanted his family exposed to Christian teachings. To make it short, he, his wife, and both children made professions of faith and were baptized—all on the same night. Today, that man is an active churchman, deacon, teacher—a pillar of his church.

Who knows, this could be Sgt. Fred Herndon. I rather believe it will be, because a sensitive chaplain knows how to meet a sensitive man.

EDITOR'S NOTE.—How would you witness to Sgt. Herndon?

8

"What's God Ever Done for Me?"

John D. Hendrix

Bill is a sullen seventeen-year-old boy built like a college football player. He spent the last three years in the adolescent ward of a state mental hospital. Although there has been some improvement, Bill still shows much antisocial behavior. The staff members asked the hospital chaplain to spend some time with Bill. The following day, Bill stormed into the chaplain's office.

Practically shouting, he said, "They said I had to come today. Why did it have to be me? A lot of guys over in my ward are not having counseling. You church guys give me the creeps. I don't have anything to say to you. I don't come to your chapel services. In fact I'm thinking about being a Catholic. Why did they make me see you?"

The next day the chaplain had a chance to examine Bill's history from the social intake records. Bill had been admitted to the hospital by the Juvenile Court in July, 1946. On May 6, he had been involved in a robbery. Later, he cashed some checks on his mother's banking account. Bill was admitted to the hospital because of a past history of auditory hallucinations and acts of physical violence.

Bill told the social worker, "I kept hearing voices saying they would beat me up and hurt me. I'll have to fight back. I'm afraid I will lose control and hurt someone without meaning to."

A look at Bill's history showed a poor developmental background. His parents were separated and divorced when Bill was five years old. A great deal of marital discord characterized Bill's early childhood. Following the divorce, Bill was allowed to spend the next summer with his father. The father then refused to let him return to the mother. A three-year-court battle over custody followed. During this time, the mother remarried and divorced again. During this second marriage, the mother became an alcoholic. At this point, Bill ran away to live with his father and stepmother but he was rejected from the home. Bill then returned to live with his mother. During the next summer, he was caught in numerous skirmishes with the law. This background brought him to the mental hospital for therapy and treatment.

At the present time, neither his mother nor father show much interest in the patient. Bill spends his evenings in a foster home and comes back to the hospital each day for a full day of school and therapy.

It took several weeks for the chaplain to develop any kind of relationship with the boy. At first, Bill was openly rebellious, using rough language and threatening the chaplain with various verbal assaults. Gradually, a relationship began to develop in spite of Bill's inability in the past to relate to anyone.

One day Bill came to the chaplain's office, sat down, lit a cigarette and said, "I wish you could get me out of that foster home. I'd rather stay here at nights instead of going back over there."

"Why?" asked the chaplain.

Bill answered: "Well, it was all right for a while. I didn't mind it for the first six months, but it gets old. We don't get along very well anymore. They just can't see that I am growing up, particularly my foster mother, the old bag. She just watches over me like some old hen. I just can't stand her anymore."

The chaplain questioned, "Do you see any similarities in your foster home and your real home?"

Bill came back with a question. "You mean with my real mother? Well, I didn't get along with her either. It seems like all my life I've been arguing with someone. Women are too bossy. They pick on you and nag at you. No one really cares about me except the people here at the hospital. I like it here. This is my home."

Only once did Bill and the chaplain talk about religion. Bill brought it up one day as they sat in the hospital cafeteria. He said, "I went to chapel today. I usually don't listen to what is going on, but today it was interesting. It's hard for me to understand anything about God. We never went to church when I was a kid. I don't guess I have been in church over five times in my life. When I used to hear those voices, I would think that God was talking to me. I was afraid and felt that God was angry at me and wanted to hurt me. Now, it just doesn't make any sense to me. You are the first person I have ever met who really believed in God. But why should I? He hasn't done anything for me."

The hospital was unsure of what direction to take with

Bill. The foster home idea was not working out. Bill's statement about women was true. His mother had forsaken him and he couldn't forget it. The hospital staff talked about a long-term treatment center which would offer Bill vocational rehabilitation. Finally, an arrangement was made for Bill to go to a vocational school in a nearby city and to live at the halfway house. The week before Bill left he had one more session with the chaplain.

"Bill, this is our last meeting," the chaplain said. "I hope that you will call me when you get over in the city. What are your plans?"

Bill answered: "Well, as I have told you I plan to go to the McClain House, starting the first of June. I have to get a job. That is the main thing."

In a voice of reassurance, the chaplain said, "You will have to let me know if I can help you."

"I'll call you when I get over there," Bill replied. "I will be going to school this fall if I can work full time this summer and part-time while I am going to school. I think I can make it."

"Why do you think you can?" queried the chaplain.

Bill answered: "Because I am better. I don't get mad like I used to. I know I can't do anything about my past. I also know that my mother and father are not going to take care of me. I don't need them, though. So I must take care of myself. Have you seen my grade card this semester?"

The chaplain said that he had not seen Bill's card but was interested in his grades.

"My grades are about twice as good as they were a year ago. I can concentrate better than I used to. I have learned how to use my time," Bill said.

"Do you remember what we said in Christian ethics about learning controls?" the chaplain questioned.

Bill's immediate reply was "I remember that you said the hospital tried to teach us controls so that when we get out of the hospital we will know how to control ourselves."

With deep concern, the chaplain continued: "Yes, I said all of us have to know what our boundaries are. That is when we can function best without getting into trouble. Do you think you can do it?"

Anxiously, Bill responded: "I sure hope so. There's just one thing that scares me. I'm not going to know how to act. I've been in the hospital since I was fourteen. The only kids I've been around are a bunch of kooks. I'm just not going to fit. When they find out that I've spent three years in a mental hospital, what then?"

After this discussion, the chaplain contacted the youth director of a church in the city. The youth director went to see Bill and invited him to the church. Bill was hesitant, but decided he would give it a try. The next Sunday, Bill, with his long, unkempt, black hair, and illfitting sport coat, walked into the Sunday School class of seventeen-year-old boys in a large suburban church.

HOW TO WIN THIS PERSON TO CHRIST

Kenneth L. Chafin . . .

Principle.—God uses many interests and many skills to bring life, healing, and hope to a person.

Paul spoke to the church at Corinth about this principle when he suggested that some planted and some watered, but God gave the increase. (See 1 Cor. 3:7.) In this particular experience, we see the science of psychiatry and the concern of a minister joining hands.

My first reaction to Bill is one of sympathy and helplessness. I have not worked with very many people who have these problems, so I have no experiences to bring to them. In addition, I have had no special clinical training in psychology, and I am wise enough to see that there are problems with which I am not capable of coping. I would imagine that this would be true of many of the people who are reading this book. And it might bring up a very important point. There are many times when we deal with people who have emotional or psychological or even physical difficulties which are affecting their spiritual difficulties. We ought to be wise enough to realize that a part of our witness concerning Jesus Christ might be to point these people to places where they can get medical attention for these problems. This in no way undermines the importance of a person's relationship to Christ. On the contrary, it dramatizes the fact that the Christian is interested in the whole person.

I see the beginning of hope for Bill in the relationship that the chaplain was willing to establish with him. This relationship was the one which seems to be laying the foundation for his improvement. The chaplain was the first adult with whom Bill identified who responded with love, concern, and understanding.

Some effort needs to be made to communicate to the pastor and those who will work with his age group about Bill's need. Young people in a church *can* be very clannish and not too prone to accept new people and have been known to be cruel and cool. It might be good for the workers to alert one or two of the more mature and more spiritually sensitive young people and solicit their help.

Bill needs to know some adults in a family relationship who will continue the acceptance and love he found from the chaplain. Right now, more than anything else, he needs to see the love of God acted out in the lives of people in relationship to him. He needs new experiences by which to understand that he is the object of God's love.

In situations like this, we are tempted to go to one of two extremes. First, we are tempted to get an easy commitment from him as a cure-all to all of his problems. Bill can commit his life to Christ now, but this will not undo all that has gone before. Second, we are tempted to rely entirely upon professional psychiatric help. The doctors can help, but the love of God is good medicine, too. The healing fellowship of a church and sound medical practice go hand in hand. It will take time, but it took time with many of us and we did not have Bill's problems.

I would think that sensitive adults, given time, will be able to lead Bill to a relationship with Christ and the type of spiritual growth that will allow him to have the life that he so desperately needs.

Our churches need to be more sensitive to the spiritual needs of children who are crippled by being in families where there is no love. There are scores of Sunday School teachers who are to some boys and girls the only adults who really loves them. We should remember that they interpret the love of God as they see us act it out.

Herschel H. Hobbs . . .

Bill is one of those unfortunate children who were *damned* for being *born* into the world. Domestic battles have left scars on his mind and heart. Fought over and rejected, it is little wonder that he ran afoul of the law. The "voices" which he heard may well have been caused by those of his father in his memory. This could explain why he related them to God. His antagonism toward his foster mother reflects his attitude toward his mother and stepmother.

Bill's first belligerent attitude toward the chaplain shows that he had declared war on the world. But patience and understanding began to pay off. Bill's growing confidence in the chaplain led him to go to chapel with an open heart. Having been denied church training he was largely bereft of spiritual influence. Yet, it was he who brought up the subject of religion in a conference following his chapel attendance. To him, the chaplain was the first person he had met "who really believed in God." Yet, Bill still could not see why he should believe in God. "He hasn't done anything for me," Bill said. Although Bill had not realized it, something had been done for him. The influence of the chaplain had begun to change his attitude.

Furthermore, arrangements were made for a change in environment. Bill was given a chance to do something for himself. He put the past behind him and faced the future with courage and hope. Recognizing the improvement that had taken place, he showed his confidence in the chaplain by promising to keep in touch.

Bill had one fear—"I'm not going to know how to act." After all, he was going into a strange, new world. However, the chain of events was kept intact through the chaplain's contact with the youth director in a church of Bill's new city. This eventually brought him to a Sunday School class of boys his age. But "his long, unkempt hair and illfitting sport coat" pose a problem. He stands out like a sore thumb. Doubtless, Bill is as much aware of this as anyone.

I am assuming that the Sunday School teacher has been informed about the situation beforehand. So what can he do to win Bill?

If I were in the teacher's place, the first thing I would do would be to get Bill to a barber. Then I would help him to get some better clothes. He must be made to fit in and to feel that he *is* in. I would counsel with the other boys in the class, urging them to let Bill know that he is accepted as one of them.

Due to his background experience, Bill must be given a sense of security. Therefore, I would make it a point to gain his confidence through between-Sundays associations. I would pray for him and teach with emphasis upon the love of God for each of the boys in the class. And I would see that each lesson had the plan of salvation.

At the proper time, I would sit down privately with Bill and talk with him about accepting Christ as his Saviour. I would dwell upon the fact that God loves him and has a wonderful plan for his life. But I would point out how because of Bill's own sinful nature God had not had his will in his life. Then I would show Bill what God, because of his love, has done in Christ for him and for all of us. I would identify myself with him as a sinner. I would tell him what Christ has meant to me since I believed in him as my Saviour. Then I would endeavor to lead Bill to receive him also. I would pray with him and ask him to pray for himself.

Then I would try to lead him to a definite commitment to Christ. If he did so, I would offer to walk down the aisle with him as he made his profession of faith in Christ. And I would continue to stay close to him as he grew in grace and knowledge of Christ.

Ordinarily, I do not think of Bill as an individual who would be won in one visit. His total background must be overcome. Because of it, Bill is suspicious of everyone. But love and patience will bear fruit as the Holy Spirit works.

G. Avery Lee . . .

Diagnosis.—Unfortunately, there are thousands of Bills (and their female counterparts), and the majority of them do not have the benefit of trained professionals. They are left to do battle with a hostile world alone. Even Bill, with the benefit of a little semiprofessional help, senses that he is not going to fit in the outside world. The hospital is the only home he has ever known—the only place where he feels that people care about him as a person.

Bill's bad experience with women gives a portent of worse things to come. Sexual perversion, sadism, or possibly even the murder of women is written in the future because so often he has been rejected by women.

I get the feeling that, despite Bill's rapport with the chaplain, the chaplain didn't put a foot in the door the one time Bill opened a wee crack to the religious room of his locked-up life. The chaplain was a bit too impersonal. This may be necessary in a counseling relationship. Bill needed a "father-image" to whom he could transfer some longings and needs. Perhaps the chaplain is not that person, but some man needs to be.

We make much of God being "Heavenly Father"; so, we may be in for trouble since Bill's father-reactions have been those of negative rejection. It will be hard for him to believe that God, the Father, loves him.

Relationship.—Bill needs, and must have, a sense of warm friendship, love, affection, and a feeling of acceptance and belonging. Who is going to give this to him? The chaplain evidently does not live in the city where Bill is to move. Perhaps the youth director of the church could give this security. Or, he could enlist the aid of some strong man, perhaps of the youthful grandfather type who could give the needed security.

The chaplain seems too impersonal and permissive in waiting for Bill to call if he needs help. He knows help will be needed. Why couldn't the chaplain have helped make arrangements for Bill to have a job waiting, instead of leaving him to find one for himself?

Prescription.—It is tragic that Bill is being turned loose in the world to go it alone. He will need professional help for a long time. This should be provided right from the beginning. Surely the church has a Christian psychiatrist or counselor, or knows one, who would do this—free!

Assuming that the right man is found to give the security relationship which has been mentioned, his wife would need careful screening, too. There is no suggesting that they take Bill into the home on a permanent basis. However, taking him hunting, to sports events, and other such occasions will help restore Bill's confidence in people.

The youth director's visit and invitation were right steps. Think of the wistful longing that gave Bill enough courage to go to Sunday School. If the youth director took time to prepare the youth group to accept Bill, he will probably return. Whatever Bill's ability—sports, music, writing—enlistment in an activity will help him feel that he belongs and has something to contribute. He has received help from others for so long that now he needs to be able to give something in return to build his confidence and self-respect.

This is no time to drill Bill between the eyes with the demands of the gospel and the plan of salvation. He needs to be aware of his sin and of his need of Christ, but only after he has confidence in the people who are telling him. His already suspicious nature and built-in rebellion will only build a stronger wall of resistance to early overt approaches. Loving patience that shows Bill that he is loved for himself is called for.

Bill will not make it with the best therapy in the world, unless he can get a *home* with powerful affection. This will include the opportunity for him to test this affection to the point of alienation. It will take a very mature couple to launch this young man. Therapy, although a must, is second on the list.

EDITOR'S NOTE.—How would you witness to this person?

9

"If They Really Knew"

Albert L. Meiburg

Phyllis Thompson's eyes are dark and sad. When we were in high school together her glances quite regularly raised male blood pressures. But that's years ago, now, and a lot has happened since then. Perhaps I see sorrow in her eyes because I know something of what she has recently been through.

After we graduated from high school Phyllis went to live with her married sister in Little Rock. She attended a business school there, and became a legal secretary. None of us back in Smithville were too surprised when we learned she had married her boss, an up-and-coming lawyer.

She kept her married name after the divorce. I guess this is why it didn't register with me when Martha Stowe, our PTA president, told me that Phyllis Dexter would serve with me on the hospitality committee. So I was a little startled at the first meeting of the year when Martha introduced her.

There wasn't much time to talk until after the meeting. Then, as we tidied up the kitchen in the strangely-quiet building we had a chance to get reacquainted. I admitted my surprise at meeting her again after these years.

"Well, Phyllis, it's nice to have you back in Smithville, again. I'm afraid you may find things a bit dull here, after living in Little Rock. Is your husband going to be starting a practice here?"

Her sad eyes avoided me as she dried a saucer.

"You haven't heard about my divorce?" she asked.

"Why, no. I'm so sorry. Forgive me."

"Don't feel badly," Phyllis interrupted. "I might as well get used to explaining things."

"Well, I didn't mean to pry," I explained. "I just wondered why you were back, and . . . and if I could do anything to help you get settled."

About a month later, having seen no sign of Phyllis at Sunday School, I renewed my invitation.

"By the way, Phyllis," I said, "I've been hoping to see you at church."

"I did bring the children a couple of Sundays," she explained. "They like it fine. I just haven't been able to stay, myself, though. Perhaps soon."

Again the following week we found ourselves collecting paper cups and brushing up the crumbs in the school kitchen.

"Did you send your pastor around to work on me about coming to church?" she asked, when things had grown quiet.

"Why, no, I didn't," I said, guessing that he had probably followed up the enrollment of Sammy and Susan in Sunday School.

"I just wondered," Phyllis continued. "I am glad for the

children to be in Sunday School, and I know it would help me to be in church, too, but somehow, it's harder for me to make the effort than I had thought it would be.

"When you first invited me, I said to myself, 'she's right. I ought to go. Perhaps I could get some answers to some questions I have.' But, when Sunday morning comes, my nerve fails.

"I keep telling myself it is a silly notion. After all, it's not as though I were going to a totally new or strange place. I've known this church for years, and although a lot of people have come and gone, there are still a lot I know . . . Perhaps that's part of the problem, like I said to the pastor: 'When you've grown up in a place, and have had Christian ideals instilled in you, and then something happens and you disappoint the very people who have tried to teach you the right, it makes it hard to come back and face them.'"

HOW TO WIN THIS PERSON TO CHRIST

Kenneth L. Chafin . . .

Principle.—The church is not a collection of the better people in the community but is made up of confessed sinners whose only hope is in Jesus Christ. Sometimes the church forgets this. When the disciples came back from buying provisions and found Jesus talking with the woman of Samaria they were somewhat incensed that she would talk with him and were curious as to why he would bother with her (John 4). The problem was that they had forgotten that the church was basically a company of confessed sinners who are trusting Christ for forgiveness. There is something wrong with the church when people whom Christ loves and for whom he died do not feel comfortable in the presence of people who have tasted his forgiveness.

Phyllis is a badly hurt individual. She suffers from a terrible sense of failure. She judges herself and will not forgive herself. Added to the burden of becoming a parent without a partner is the crisis of re-entry into her own hometown. Perhaps she remembers how she had felt about girls whose marriages did not work out. Perhaps she remembers catty little things that she listened to and participated in in discussing these girls and their trouble. In all likelihood divorced people are more common than she thinks. And people may be much more understanding than she anticipates. There are few families today who do not have some person related to them who has experienced the hurt and frustration of a marriage that has failed.

The attitude that individuals take toward her will be of tremendous importance. She needs assurance about herself. She needs someone to help her with her son. She needs some time away from a five-year-old. She needs some adult friends. She needs acceptance. Eventually she needs to discover what it means to be forgiven and to forgive oneself. She needs to know the healing power of the Holy Spirit of God. She needs individuals who really care for her in a series of contacts. Time is an important factor. A marriage does not fall apart overnight and lives do not heal easily. If she has several friends who will spend time with her without pushing it will help her to be relaxed back home.

She cannot start over and undo everything, but God is willing to take her where she is and begin at this spot. The person needs to help her see that life must not ultimately get its approval from environment. She needs a sense of inner faith that makes it possible for her to live in a context where everyone does not approve of her.

It is a very rare church that does not have some active member who has had the tragedy of a broken home. I think that it would be good to get one of these individuals to assume a responsibility to help her find her way into the life of the church again. This is not an impossible thing. This is such a critical period in her life. The type of community and the type of love and the type of hope that is held out in the church is desperately needed by this woman.

In my pastorate in seminary we were able to win many parents of Beginner and Primary age children by our ministry to the child. The child is all she has left. When the church helps the child it opens a way to help her help herself.

If she cannot be reached by her home church she might enjoy a newer church where she would not be so constantly reminded of the past. The important thing is reaching her, not in getting her in a certain church.

G. Avery Lee . . .

Diagnosis: We know something about Phyllis Thompson Dexter's present situation, and a little of her youth, but relatively nothing about the Little Rock years of her married life. All we know is that her husband was a "ladies' man." (His choice?) She feels she had scriptural grounds for divorce. Her husband's rough house play with Sammy indicates some love for the children.

We can sense in Phyllis a mood of inadequacy, despair, and resignation. She does not give herself the right to be a person, but lets others pass judgment. In this mood she will not respond to the "hard sell," but can be motivated only by warmth, even before light.

Relationship: As usual, acceptance and love will be key factors. Phyllis is not the first, nor will she be the last divorcee in Smithville. In the small town there is less chance to be anonymous, and there is more chance of being snubbed. The city is but the town writ large, with more total, but perhaps no higher percentage of divorces, or other problems.

If she is as attractive as she once was, some of the

women might feel her a threat, remembering the tales of "The Gay Divorcee." And some of the more predatory males, remembering the same thing, may think her fair game.

Phyllis' feeling that she can "come home" is good. Feeling loved by her parents and accepted by them will give her some stability. Also, despite not having Daddy, the children will be given grandparental love. She will need someone with whom she can talk. Let's hope the pastor is such a person, as well as her PTA friend. Can we find a man, just for companionship at dinner, a show, or a ball game?

Prescription: A frank talk with the Sunday School class about Phyllis is in order. The members can become aware of her needs and of their responsibility of accepting her without "stone throwing."

The pastor is the focal person in this case. A talk with him to ascertain his feelings about divorced persons and how he accepts them is called for. His attitude will go far in determining overall church reaction. If he is a stern legalist, we are in for trouble.

Even in a small town there may be enough divorced persons to have, or begin, a Parents Without Partners club, where men and women with similar problems and understandings can get together. The church facilities could be made available in the beginning.

Phyllis is right, most social affairs are planned with couples in mind. Why not have one where the "unattached" are invited, not to play cupid, but to get people together. She will need, and probably want some masculine attention, without thought of romantic involvement.

Phyllis already feels that the church considers her a sinner because of her divorce. She feels she has let people down. She needs to feel that divorce in itself is not a sin. Here is an opportunity for the church to get under her load and help bear her burden. In the attitude of acceptance, God's love and forgiveness gets across. It is easier to accept the forgiveness of another than it is to forgive one's self. Also, it will be hard for her to forgive her husband. But this all around forgiveness is available and necessary.

In "nosing around" we might see if there is any possible chance of reconciliation with Mr. Dexter, even as there is reconciliation with God.

Herschel H. Hobbs . . .

From the case description I assume that Phyllis Thompson or Mrs. Dexter is a Christian who hesitates to affiliate with the local church because of an unfortunate marriage which ended in a divorce. So the problem here is to lead her to realize her need and to seek for the church and its ministry to her and her two children.

In dealing with Phyllis one must remember that she has suffered a traumatic experience. Regardless of the cause a divorce is always a tragic thing. And in the case at hand it is especially true of Phyllis. This is so because of the Christian ideals which were instilled in her as a child. It is evident that she had taken her marriage vows seriously. And now she feels that she has disappointed those who love and trust her. So she is a victim of self-incrimination. She even imagines that people are saying unkind things behind her back. This may be partly true. But it is also possible that she imagines more than is the case. This is compounded by her sense of inadequacy to meet the needs of her children, especially her son.

First, I would explain to her Jesus' teaching about divorce. In Matthew 19 where He said, "What therefore God hath joined together, let no man put asunder," He also said, "Whosoever shall put away his wife [or husband], except it be for fornification." From her own statement Phyllis admitted that her husband "was such a ladies' man." In this light I would seek to show her that she had New Testament grounds for divorce. What happened was not her fault. To be sure, she had suffered because of it. But that is all the more reason for her to seek help in putting together again the pieces of her broken life.

But having said all of this, I am aware that Phyllis' trouble is that "when Sunday morning comes, my nerve fails." Therefore, instead of inviting her to Sunday School and church, I would arrange to go by and take her and her children the next Sunday morning. And I would offer to go forward with her in the church service as she finds affiliation, fellowship, and love in the company of the redeemed.

WHO'S WHO

Kenneth L. Chafin is Billy Graham Professor of Evangelism, The Southern Baptist Theological Seminary, Louisville, Kentucky.

Harold E. Dye is pastor, Baptist Temple, San Jose, California.

John D. Hendrix is editor of Young People's materials, Training Union Department, Baptist Sunday School Board, Nashville, Tennessee.

Herschel H. Hobbs is pastor, First Baptist Church, Oklahoma City, Oklahoma.

Clifford Ingle is professor of religious education and church administration, Midwestern Baptist Theological Seminary, Kansas City, Missouri.

John A. Ishee is editor of Adult materials, Training Union Department, Baptist Sunday School Board, Nashville, Tennessee.

G. Avery Lee is pastor, St. Charles Avenue Baptist Church, New Orleans, Louisiana.

Albert L. Meiburg is chaplain-supervisor, Crozer-Chester Medical Center, Chester, Pennsylvania.

W. T. Moore is secretary of inter-racial ministries, Baptist Convention of Michigan, Detroit.

Jack D. Sanford is pastor, First Baptist Church, Florence, Kentucky.

William L. Self is pastor, Wieuca Road Baptist Church, Atlanta, Georgia.

John Warren Steen, Jr. is pastor, First Baptist Church, Clayton, North Carolina.